THE SILENT SEDUCTION OF SELF-TALK

THE SILENT SEDUCTION OF SELF-TALK

CONFORMING DEADLY THOUGHT PATTERNS TO THE WORD OF GOD

SHELLY BEACH

MOODY PUBLISHERS
CHICAGO

Published in association with the literary agency of Credo Communications, LLC, Grand Rapids, MI 49525.

Editor: Pam Pugh
Inside Design: Ragont Design
Cover Illustrations and Design: Maralynn Rochat

Library of Congress Cataloging-in-Publication Data

Beach, Shelly.
The silent seduction of self-talk : conforming deadly thought patterns to the Word of God / by Shelly Beach.
p. cm.
Includes bibliographical references.
ISBN 978-0-8024-5077-7
1. Christian women—Religious life. 2. Self-talk—Religious aspects—Christianity. 3. Beach, Shelly. I. Title.
BV4527.B39 2009
248.4—dc22

2008051902

This book is printed on acid free recycled paper containing 30% PCW (Post Consumer Waste) and manufactured in the United States of America by Bethany Press.

We hope you enjoy this book from Moody Publishers. Our goal is to provide high-quality, thought-provoking books and products that connect truth to your real needs and challenges. For more information on other books and products written and produced from a biblical perspective, go to www.moodypublishers.com or write to:

Moody Publishers
820 N. LaSalle Boulevard
Chicago, IL 60610

1 3 5 7 9 10 8 6 4 2

Printed in the United States of America

To Louie and Mona Konopka
who model how to listen,
how to speak,
and how to love

Contents

The Story Behind

Silent Seduction

The concept for this book took shape a few years ago as I was driving through a blizzard scribbling on a notepad propped on my steering wheel. (Since then I have repented of such craziness, and my husband has bought me a voice recorder.) But even as ideas poured from me, fear poked through my thoughts like thistles in newly seeded grass.

Not fear that I would skid across the median or plow through a drainage ditch, but fear of the inevitability of pain—the same fear that had settled over me the first time I'd learned I was pregnant.

I have never been a fan of pain.

Perhaps you can empathize with me. Imagine if I asked you to insert an electronic device in your brain and record your self-talk for the next few months, then share your jealousies, insecurities, manipulations, secret judgments, prejudices, and pretensions on the printed page for the world to read. Would you wave your hand in the air to volunteer?

I wasn't sure I wanted to coax my hand into the air either. But that was the kind of book I was envisioning—one that shared the guts and the glory of my struggle with destructive self-talk. But then, I wasn't so sure anyone would want to read about my journey in the first place. After all, I'm not a psychologist or an expert on much of anything except how to set off a smoke alarm when attempting to cook. It's true that I'm a Christian educator with a seminary degree and a few book contracts here and there. A speaker, even, and a Sunday school teacher who at one time had so many perfect attendance pins I could string them together and tuck them into my belt. But my credential for writing this book was going to be the fact that I'd somehow deceived myself for most of my life.

This book idea wouldn't let me go, though. I figured if I'd plowed through life well-intentioned but self-deceived, other people must, too. Deceiving ourselves through our self-talk is part of what Scripture implies when it says that "the heart is deceitful above all things and beyond cure. Who can understand it?" (Jeremiah 17:9). So I pushed on, shoving away my fears, fairly certain that publishers wouldn't be interested in what I had to say. After all, I'd never written a bestseller, and the last time I'd checked, I didn't have a television or radio show. And then one day my agent called and announced that Moody Publishers had decided to help me birth this book, and I knew I had no choice but to face the pain of trying to write about parts of me I'd rather not let people see.

This book is about facing who we are on the inside, even when we don't want to look. For this reason, it was impossible for me to write without spilling my personal struggles onto the pages. They're there to help you see the daily war we wage in our self-talk. The truth we choose to believe shapes our attitudes toward our circumstances, our goals, and our relationships with our bosses, spouses, children, friends, ourselves, and most important, with God.

This book is based on the foundational assumption that the Bible is inerrant and authoritative, and its truth can be known. That starting point provides the paradigm from which I apply principles from the Word of God to life.

Second, this book is my journey, written to encourage readers in growing in their relationship with God. It's a book about God's precious gift of change. One means of pursuing change is by studying what we tell ourselves. As the title suggests, this book centers on recognizing our negative self-talk and aligning our thoughts to biblical truth.

As a word of explanation, it's extremely difficult to describe the nature of thoughts. I don't know about yours, but mine don't always proceed in a linear fashion. So understand that I've taken a bit of creative license when presenting my inner conversations. My actual thoughts are often fairly scattered but the essence of my struggles have been retained—often from notes from my journal.

Some of the most valuable elements of this book are the interactive materials at the end of each chapter and in the appendices. These materials were developed to help you personally apply the chapter concepts and explore your own self-talk as you seek discernment and wisdom. Prayerfully consider working through these exercises, as well as journaling as you study your own thought processes.

My prayer for each of you is this: May your love "abound more and more in knowledge and depth of insight, so that you may be able to discern what is best and may be pure and blameless until the day of Christ, filled with the fruit of righteousness that comes through Jesus Christ—to the glory and praise of God" (Philippians 1:9–11).

—Shelly Beach

CHAPTER 1

SLATHER *Me Up and Stuff Me In:*

How an MRI Exposed the Me I Never Wanted to Know

Before I can live with other folks I've got to live with myself. The one thing that doesn't abide by majority rule is a person's conscience.

—Atticus Finch in Harper Lee's *To Kill a Mockingbird*

Seduction has many voices. It calls in strident tones and wears a painted face, luring us boldly with lust, desire, and pride.

And it beckons in the silent spaces of apathy that linger between our motives and words. Like an anaconda, it lurks beneath the watermark of consciousness, waiting to grip us in its diabolical embrace, then slowly crush the life from us.

THE SERPENT BENEATH

For most of my adult life, I'd stood waist-deep in water, seduced by superficial ripples of apathy, unaware that seduction had coiled around me. I didn't know a monster existed in the waters of my life. I'd chosen delusion, and my monster of delusion was my own self-talk, a reality that lurked beneath the waterline of my awareness. I'd ignored it and slipped into blissful apathy regarding its power in my life. Mine was a silent seduction.

Until the day my body and soul slammed into an insurmountable wall of need, and I found myself eavesdropping on my heart for the first time.

One minute I was hurtling full-throttle down the road of life, radio blaring and windows rolled up tight to the world around me while I steered with my knee and scribbled church committee meetings into my planner. Then suddenly my face was planted in gravel and grit, and darkness had swallowed me.

It was the kind of crash that leaves permanent skid marks on your soul, the kind that divides your life into *Before* and *After.* But I never saw it coming. I was too busy careening from task to task on a full tank of premium self-obsession that was propelling me through life like a pinball on steroids.

Don't get me wrong. I was doing all the right things—the admirable things Christians tell themselves they do to honor God. I was just doing them for the wrong reasons and didn't know it. I hadn't learned to listen to my self-talk yet. I'd mastered plenty of ways to hide my true motives from myself. After all, my husband, Dan, and I had worked in full-time Christian ministry for over twenty years, and nobody I knew was sitting around church potluck suppers talking about their secret agendas or roots of bitterness. Besides, Dan and I had a solid marriage and two phenomenal adult children. I was teaching, writing, speaking, serving. I had the day planner to prove I was doing things of eternal value, and if I could bring it along to heaven for a little celestial Show-and-Tell someday, I was sure I'd outshine many of my friends.

After all, I'd directed small church choirs, community choirs, *junior high* choirs, for heaven's sake (I'd always assumed an extra dollop of God's blessing anywhere junior highers were involved). And then there were the high school mission trips that involved tarantulas and honest-to-goodness deprivation and outhouses and manual labor in the desert. I was practically one with Corrie ten Boom and Mother Teresa on those trips. To my way of thinking, of course, before I learned to turn up the volume on thoughts I hadn't wanted to admit were there.

And then there was the tiny salary we'd lived on and the hundreds of kids whose lives we'd poured ourselves into. According to my Subconscious Spiritual Checklist, I was doing all right. I was in ministry leadership, and I smiled most of the time in public and tried hard to have devotions and feel appropriately guilty when I didn't. Like a lot of people I knew, I'd come to believe that spiritual growth was measured by not complaining too much and banging out the jobs on my Christian to-do list. I thought I had a bright, shiny heart, buffed up and polished, like some kind of spiritual gazing ball. On good days, if I kept myself busy enough, I actually believed it.

When there were doubts, I shoved them aside and took more notes in church. Doubts were to be ignored. Doubts were signs of spiritual weakness and cracks in the armor of God, and I did not want to be cracked.

And so I ran faster, jumped higher, scribbled more commitments into my planner, and kept my Christian radio station turned up loud enough to cover the babble that raged below the surface of my soul.

It wasn't until I slammed into an insurmountable wall of need that I began to see that the bright places in my heart were only mirages, glimmers of heat rising from the parched soil of my soul that had gone dry years ago.

But my need would become God's megaphone. Pain would force me to lie still with my eyes squeezed shut and my face planted in dirt as I searched for God's perspective—a perspective that I'd buried beneath layers of rationalization, excuse, pride, fear, and my compulsion to please.

My acts of service had been self-service to impress people.

My hands extended in missions had been grasping to prove to those around me that I was willing to do "spiritual" things, difficult things.

My loyalties and commitment to friends had often been fear of rejection wrapped in the tinsel of approval addiction.

Until my life slammed into a wall of physical pain and suffering, I hadn't known these things about myself, at least in ways I was willing to admit. I hadn't known them because I'd never learned to listen to the whisperings of my own heart. I'd smothered the sound of my own soul crying out for soul fulfillment.

Perhaps it was the knowledge deep within me that I was truly broken, truly needy that kept me racing from task to task, anesthetizing my emptiness with the next date scribbled into my planner. Something inside me told me that as long as I was moving, I didn't have to focus on where I really was, on who I really was.

He pressed my face so close to His own that I finally saw glimmers of my real self for the very first time reflected in His eyes.

In June of 1999, God decided to introduce me to myself. It was the month when my self-obsession collided with His love, and He pressed my face so close to His own that I finally saw glimmers of my real self for the very first time reflected in His eyes. It was the month when I first began to hear the whisperings of my true neediness and the voice of God calling me to Himself.

A journey was about to begin, a journey that would end with me, Shelly Beach, meeting myself for the first time. But before it would begin, I would have to slam into that wall of suffering and stare into the dirt for a while.

And it would hurt.

COLLIDING WITH GOD

I began to hear the squeal of the brakes and feel the seat belt tighten against my chest during an unnerving emergency room discussion with a doctor who wanted to crank off my skull to root around inside my brain. I'd just returned from a trip to Europe, so I was accustomed to knowing my legs would take me from point A to point B. But two days after I'd returned home, I woke up to find my legs had gone on strike. I was suddenly unable to support my own weight, much less walk, and so one afternoon Dan carried me into a hospital emergency room like the world's largest rag doll.

Within hours, all parts of me were refusing to cooperate. Apparently, I was considered an interesting specimen and was offered every test available, then promptly shipped off to a new hospital farther up the food chain. Twice.

Soon after arriving at Detroit Medical Center, I was tied up with my bedsheets and slid into an MRI tube. This was not the welcome I'd been hoping for. Perhaps this technique was for ease of stuffing or the technicians were afraid that once they slid me in, they wouldn't be able to slide me back out. But I did find it frightening that none of the self-avowed medical professionals buzzing around me that day recognized the terrifying implications of tying up a patient producing frequent and violent gastric expulsions and shoving her into a space half her size. But they'd been given the job of determining if the Giant Thing Near My Brain Stem was a real-live tumor, and I'd already been given maximum doses of every antinausea medication known to medical science. So their only recourse was to stuff me in the tube, repeat polite platitudes, do the Hokey Pokey, and hope for the best.

I had already earned, in my brief stay in the neuro-oncology unit at Detroit Medical Center, the much-deserved name of the "Puking Lady in Room 332." But despite my impressive credentials, I was not offered a free pass for the test where technicians encase your head inside a giant helmet screwed to a sliding MRI table. I was certain that if I had been a schnauzer or a guinea pig, animal rights activists would have protected me from such an abomination. I could see through one slitted eye that the people in white intended to tie me down, clamp me in, and stuff my larger-than-pimento-sized girth into an olive-sized tube. I have never been good at geometry, but even in my diminished mental state, I knew I was in serious trouble.

The most important reason was that I hadn't opened my eyes in days. My universe had come to resemble a kaleidoscope of bouncing, trembling, triplicate blobs that had forced me into a fetal position while I prayed that no one weighing more than a Chihuahua would walk any closer than my door. I wanted people to stop blowing up my veins and sticking pins in my legs and writing in ink on my chart that I couldn't stand up or walk or keep my eyeballs from jerking like a hummingbird on caffeine. I wanted them to stop reminding me that life had suddenly, inexplicably spun out of control because a walnut-sized something-or-other had taken up residence near my brain stem. I wanted them to figure out what it was and how to get rid of it so they could get me out of that horrible hospital and back to my *life*, which was disintegrating with the ticking of the clock.

And to top it off, a radiologist who had not been taught that Customer Satisfaction Is Number One had told me that I would have to lie absolutely still on my back for over an hour to get the images that would determine if life as I had known it would ever resume. For a fleeting second I'd considered laughing. Lying on my back for even ten minutes would have required a miracle on par with my performing with the Bolshoi Ballet, but no one seemed interested in what I could or couldn't do. They were only interested in what I *had* to do.

A panic ball was placed in my right hand as the sheets were pulled taut, then tied over my chest.

"I can't do this. I'm going to throw up in there."

"You've got the panic ball. If you feel sick, give it a squeeze, and we'll pull you out."

I was slid onto the narrow table as the tech maneuvered my head into the helmet, and I felt the locking mechanism click into place. With the sound, a prayer rose from deep within me.

Dear God. I can't do this.

"You'll be all right, ma'am. MRIs really aren't a big deal. All you have to do is close your eyes, think peaceful thoughts, and be still."

THE THUD OF THE SOUL

My heart sank as I felt the thud of my soul hitting a wall.

Be still.

Now there was a concept I'd never been able to grasp. I'd floundered with it for years, even though I'd done the right things my pastors had preached about. Devotions, praying, and always I'd felt the thud of my soul hitting that wall.

With a gentle whirring, I felt the table move and my shoulders curl as my body cupped to the shape of the cylinder.

The first grip of panic tore at my chest. A soft current brushed my face, yet I felt as if the air had been sucked from my lungs. Cold metal pressed against me, and I squeezed my eyes shut so tightly I feared my blood vessels might burst. I knew that if my lids flickered open for only an instant and I glimpsed the cold metal encasing me like a coffin, I would scream. A single question pounded through my mind.

Why am I here, God?

The narrowness of the space pressed in. I was trapped. I could do nothing but lie still and wait. I inhaled and tried to ignore the pressure of the sheets shrouding me.

I don't know how to do this, God. I'm not strong enough. You made some people strong and I am not one of them, so just hand this assignment off to someone else. I pass.

Spasms of nausea gripped my stomach. I inhaled deeply and concentrated on the light show flashing on the back of my eyelids.

"How long have I been in here?"

My voice was barely loud enough to whisper.

"It's only been twelve minutes, Mrs. Beach. You're doing fine."

This person was obviously not in the tube. I was not doing fine, and I was about to prove it. I squeezed the ball. Over and over. But it was too late.

I proved them all wrong in one terrifying spasm of horror. My head strained at the helmet, and the metal bit into my skin as I fought against my coffin. I'd tried to be still, but it hadn't been enough.

Shame washed over me as I felt the rush of hands to pull me from the tube, release my head, and clean me. If I'd had any spare body fluids, I would have cried. Because I'd failed, the doctors would have no answers. They'd be forced to make me repeat the test.

I was wheeled into the hallway where the sounds of life swirled around me as I lay in a surreal limbo with my eyes shut tight to the world. Dan joined me, and the warmth of his hand enveloped mine as he gently avoided the IVs and tubes that had become part of me.

New despair seeped into my soul as I lay again in a fetal position, my husband stroking my brow as we waited for news of nothing. In the anguish of those moments, the voices that had lay submerged beneath the watermark of my soul floated slowly to the surface.

You were only in the scanner for minutes. You faced that humiliation for nothing.

Guilt and anger washed over me, and I searched for a verse, for a thread of hope.

You're alone. You can't feel God, can you? You came out the same Shelly you went in—a bit damper and colder, but the same. They think you have cancer, you know. God doesn't promise to protect you.

Almost instantaneously, a verse sprang to mind. *But His grace is sufficient for me, and His strength is made perfect in my weakness.*

The clash of voices pulled at my thoughts.

God was with me. He's real, in spite of what I feel. He's going to provide everything I'm going to need.

God's presence is an illusion. You're not strong enough for this, and you're on your own. This is going to break your faith. You've got nothing but empty religion.

WHOSE VOICE WAS THAT?

In that moment, the world faded away. Then quietly, a parallel awareness stirred in my thoughts. I was arguing with myself. How strange was that? I was actually telling myself conflicting things that couldn't possibly both be true.

I slowly pulled myself back from the struggle and surveyed my self-talk. What I saw shocked me. For the first time I saw with clarity the lies that were raging against truth. I could see that the battle in my mind was almost like watching Atticus Finch take on Mr. Gilmer in a sweltering Alabama courtroom in *To Kill a Mockingbird.* Until that moment, I'd been unaware that I argued with myself, even lied to myself. Although my belief system and values were derived from the things I determined to be true inside my head, I'd never purposefully eavesdropped on my self-talk before. I'd ignored this internal world. Now, suddenly, an MRI scan had exposed my inner duplicity and the fact that life had kept me so focused upon my external world that my inner dialogues had been lost beneath the waterlines of my daily activity.

I'd become so busy doing the stuff of life that I'd blocked out the diabolical self-talk that marked the struggles in my own heart.

I stared into the darkness as I faced the reality that the God I'd claimed to know and to love was, in many ways, a stranger to me. It was a brutal truth to face as I waited to be taken back to the brain cancer unit. It was a truth that took me to the end of myself, and that is where the work of God began—helping me discover the parched soil of my heart, my hidden agendas and self-centered obsessions. But God had brought me to a place where I'd begin to listen, to recognize His voice, then begin to see myself, one glimpse at a time, as I found myself in Him.

I'd begin by recognizing that I battled with the desire to silence God's voice with my own.

I'd begin by recognizing that my spirit was opposed to God's, that I struggled to outwit Him, to equal Him, and ultimately become my own god. But these were truths I refused to allow to rise above the waterline of my heart until I'd learned to listen to my self-talk.

GOD'S GRACE IN A VERY SMALL SPACE

On that day in 1999 in the hospital hallway, the sound of footsteps approached.

"We're taking you back to your room, Mrs. Beach. We managed somehow to get the images of your brain we needed, right down to the second you got sick. Your doctor will be sharing the results with you, but let's just say we won't be needing a scan of your whole body after all."

Dan and I sat in stunned silence struggling to understand what we'd just been told. The truth dawned in scattered shards of hope, then in one brilliant burst.

They hadn't found a tumor or cancer. They weren't going to repeat the scan.

On a hospital gurney, surrounded by blurred shapes and clinging to a plastic basin, I heard the smallest of whispers. The voice I'd waited for in the small space of the MRI tube breathed truth quietly into my heart.

I was with you, Shelly. I always am and I always have been, even in the still, small places.

I began to listen and to hear. God's megaphone of suffering was beginning to teach me that my self-talk had obscured His voice. Unless I learned to listen in the silent spaces that lingered between my motives and my words, my soul would never find satisfaction in God alone, and I would never learn to love others.

For most of my adult life I'd been seduced by my own self-talk—seduced by spiritual apathy, by the power of delusion. I'd chosen to ignore the reality of conflicting voices vying to control my mind, will, emotions, and to place a stranglehold on my relationship with God. My compassionate, gracious, loving heavenly Father, more than anything, longed for me to know Him. For years

He'd been speaking to me, but my babbling had obscured His voice.

And so He broke my heart so that I could hear Him, so that He could lift my face to His own and draw me to Himself. For weeks, I lay in silence. And in the silent spaces of my apathy I discovered agendas, calluses, fears, and facades.

In my months of illness and recovery from my brain lesion, not a tumor, God's voice stirred fresh in me—this time a new message: "Be a woman of one voice, with pure motives and a heart for only Me."

The promise of truth flowed through me with Holy Spirit power.

Tears of brokenness softened the parched soil of my heart as I cried out to know a God who spoke to me and moved in me.

In the months that I lay in the stillness of a hospital room, I learned to listen to the silent motives of my heart. I learned that seduction wears many faces and that God's look of compassion bears only one face—the face of Jesus Christ, God's Son, who calls to us.

"Come to Me."

SOUL SEARCH
Breaking the Silence

- Do you struggle with busyness that keeps you from listening to your heart and focusing on your relationship with God? Why?
- What "bricks" can you identify in your wall of spiritual need? What attitudes, thoughts, sins, habits do you struggle to hide, even from yourself? What conversations do you have with yourself to justify or rationalize your actions?
- If you struggle with guilt in your self-talk, how does Satan use that guilt to beat you down? Do you feel it's true guilt or false guilt? Why?
- Do you struggle with feeling you truly know God? Do you desire to know Him more intimately? Can you identify what you believe may be obstacles to intimacy with God?
- Do you have a difficult time believing that God desires a personal relationship with you? What do you think may have contributed to this feeling?

Facing the Seduction
Listening to the Spirit and the Word

- Spend time in prayer asking God to reveal areas of spiritual need in your life. You may want to use one or several of the following Scripture passages or refer to the topical listing of Scripture in appendix 7.

Psalm 51
Galatians 5:22–24
Matthew 5:44–45
Matthew 16:24–26
2 Peter 1:4–8
Matthew 16:12, 14–15

- What do these passages say about God's desire to be in an intimate relationship with us?

Jeremiah 29:11
Deuteronomy 26:18
1 John 3:1
John 10:14–15
Ephesians 1:4–6

- Turn to the back of this book and complete the exercise in appendix 1.
- Consider asking an accountability partner to join you as you read through this book. Spiritual transformation is always best accomplished in conjunction with the Word of God, the Spirit of God, and the people of God. This person should be someone of spiritual maturity and discernment who knows you well enough to give loving feedback.

Responding from the Heart
Prayer

Gracious and loving Father, I come to You admitting that I'm facing a wall of need. I know that more than anything, You want to have a closer and deeper relationship with me, and today I'm taking a first step toward You by asking You to change me from the inside out. Thank You for loving me as I am but for not leaving me in my brokenness.

Please help me see the ugly parts of myself I've worked so hard to hide with self-talk. Show me who You created me to be, fully empowering me through Your Holy Spirit to become that person. Show me the roots of my self-deceptions, whether big or small. Help me listen to the conversations I carry on with myself, knowing they're a mirror to my heart, a key to my motives, and the source of my commitment to live out the double love command to passionately love You and others.

Thank You for grace and for the gift of Your love as I turn toward You in humble obedience. More than anything, Lord, I want to have a heart that loves You more. Amen.

CHAPTER 2

The MONSTER *Within:*

Tuning In to the Voices of Self-Talk

Many of our thoughts aren't helpful . . .
How much of what we say to ourselves helps
us live a better life?

—David J. Pollay, author, syndicated columnist,
host of *The Happiness Answer* television show

Among its many memorable characters, *The Cosby Show* featured a fast-talking teenager named Kara who could chatter at the speed of light. This young lady approached conversations with the finesse of a verbal blast furnace. Whenever Kara spoke, I'd inhale and wait for her to take a breath so my brain could catch up with the verbal hailstorm that flew from her lips. But try as I might, I couldn't make my mind work fast enough to keep up with this young woman who'd mastered the art of speaking as fast as she could produce outrageously random thoughts.

OUR INNER BLABBERMOUTH

According to David J. Pollay, the average person speaks at approximately 200 words per minute but thinks at more than six times that speed—1,300 words per minute. At this rate we produce approximately 45,000 thoughts per day, some worth sharing, and some about as exciting as that strange stain on our garage floor.[1]

Thoughts are our primary means of communication—with others, ourselves, and God. Try to think of a time when you communicated without producing thoughts. The very idea is an oxymoron. God designed us to express our thoughts, for the most part, in the form of words. The moment He created us in the garden of Eden, He began speaking to us, knowing we'd talk back by means of speech produced in our thoughts that often reached our lips. He designed us so words would shape our emotions, feelings, and ideas through internal thought processes and so the words we formed would be our primary tools of communication. From the moment He created us, our Creator knew that our thoughts, which He tied to our hearts and our motives, would find their way to our tongues, whether for good or for bad.

> *The good man brings good things out of the good stored up in his heart, and the evil man brings evil things out of the evil stored up in his heart. For out of the overflow of his heart his mouth speaks.*
>
> —LUKE 6:45

Whether we're waking or sleeping, silent or speaking, we're producing thoughts that exceed our tongue's ability to keep up. We're often acutely aware of the thoughts racing in our heads—for instance, when we're standing at a podium in front of a crowd fumbling for words. But at other times we're virtually ignorant of the tumble of ideas, responses, attitudes, and emotions that determine the direction of our choices and actions. And often, we allow our thoughts to shape us, rather than consciously choosing to shape our thoughts. Consequently, we ignore the fact that our mind often becomes a battleground between truth and lies. But engaging in battle assumes we understand the nature of opposing sides and of strategy.

Our most strategic battles are battles of the heart, and as they rage, we often distract ourselves from our true motives, rationalizing that our real problems must be the size of our paycheck, the size of our clothes, our grouchy neighbor, our spouse's disrespect, our lack of a spouse, culture's fixation on spouses, or that annoying parent/teacher/sibling/boss.

The apostle Paul describes our battle in the book of Romans.

> *When I want to do good, evil is right there with me. For in my inner being I delight in God's law; but I see another law at work in the members of my body, waging war against the law of my mind and making me a prisoner of the law of sin at work within my members. What a wretched man I am! Who will rescue me from this body of death? Thanks be to God—through Jesus Christ our Lord!*
>
> —Romans 7:21–25

Evil has clung to our thoughts from Adam and Eve's first encounter with Satan in the garden of Eden, and his strategy hasn't changed since his first seduction.

Doubt God's character, His good intentions, and what He says.

Put your agenda and your ideas first.

Convince yourself your alternate reality is better than God's. It's the silent seduction that led Adam and Eve straight down a path to doubting God in the garden of Eden. A battle for truth raged inside their minds, and they never even heard the clamor.

It began with a shadow of doubt, with rationalization and self-protection. It began in the silence of self-talk.

THE BLAME GAME

I sat at my desk at the Christian school where I served as dean of students. A mother stood at the counter interacting with one of our secretaries, explaining in vibrant, echoing tones why school policies regarding tardiness didn't apply to *her* daughter.

To boil it down, this mom believed her daughter was entitled to live by different rules than those set in place for other students. The rule was ridiculous and should be taken out of the handbook. High schoolers should be treated like adults and be responsible for their own attendance, as long as their parents agreed. The school was overstepping its boundaries. This mother's sense of entitlement permeated her thinking and every parental decision she made during her daughter's short tenure at our school.

Somewhere deep within this mom's heart, her self-talk had convinced her that her daughter should be treated preferentially, and she'd listened. When evidence was given to the contrary by teachers or administrators, she discarded it. Did this mother think she was harming her daughter by diverting natural consequences that would face her in the real world? No. Did she think her rationale for allowing her daughter to bypass authority was unbiblical? Not at all. She was in a position of leadership at a Bible-teaching church, and she believed good mothers should share her decision-making model for their children.

THE SEDUCTION

This mom was like most of us. She'd convinced herself that when it came to boundaries, we can pick and choose for ourselves. She'd been deceived with the same seduction that had lured Adam and Eve in the garden of Eden—first the sense and then the belief that we're deserving of rights and privileges apart from those designated by God. Entitlement is born in each of our hearts the moment soul satisfaction in God is swallowed by self-satisfaction.

In those moments that Adam and Eve pondered their actions, they convinced themselves they had no reason to operate by the rules God had set into motion. They chose to circumvent God's created order to acquire knowledge and power, the promise of a better life. In those first moments of doubt, driving forces birthed accusation on the character of God, and a demanding spirit was born in the hearts of mankind. From that moment, we as children of Adam and

Eve have demanded all we can get from our Father, from our first cry to our dying breaths, with clenched fists and defiant spirits.

Did God really say?

With those words, Satan gave birth to doubt, and to doubt, a demanding spirit, and the monster of sin was born in Eve's heart as the second act of creation was accomplished in the garden—the birth of sin in the heart of man with the skewing of his thoughts and motives. In that split second, our first parents became slaves to the monster that would ravage their souls and drag them to depths of sin beyond comprehension.

DISTRACTION AND SUBTLETY

Eve didn't seem surprised to find a snake in her garden when we first see the two together in Genesis chapter 3. Some scholars even suggest they appear to be picking up their conversation somewhere in the middle. But one surprising element of Eve's interaction with the serpent is that he never urged her to *do* anything. He simply asked her to think. With a carefully nuanced phrase or two, the serpent set Eve's self-talk in motion.

We, too, are oblivious to the capacity for evil in our lives.

Who was God anyway? What had He really said to her? Could she trust Him?

The battle of all time raged in Eve's mind as she weighed the answers. She lost, the same way we, her children, lose the same battle every day.

We, too, are oblivious to the capacity for evil in our lives.
Blind to the consequences of our choices.
Unaware of our grasping nature.
Deaf to the battle for truth that rages in our minds.

Adam and Eve were first seduced in the privacy of their thoughts, and so are we. They lost sight of the fulfillment in God that was already theirs. Our sole defense is to step back, to turn up the volume on our thoughts, to evaluate them, and to begin acting on truth.

GETTING DOWN AND DIRTY WITH THE MONSTER

This is the part of the book where I'd like to insert a hard-hitting example from someone else's life, but God has told me to write where I fight. Unfortunately, I fight in some pretty stinky trenches. I think we all do.

About four years ago, Dan and I began going to a marriage counselor—not because our marriage was in trouble but because I sensed that after thirty or so years of marriage, I'd become someone who was pretty yucky to live with. Yucky is a nice word, but I'll leave it at that.

On the surface, Dan and I looked like a great couple. We smiled a lot, had seminary degrees, and held hands in public. We seldom argued because I was always right. This made things easy. About six hours into our marriage, Dan realized he'd never win an argument unless I went into a coma. So he'd simply crawled into his compliant, gracious self, while I honed the fine arts of manipulation and sarcasm (all in good fun, right?).

Dan and I coasted along in our state of marital oblivion for nearly three decades, like many couples we knew, not thinking about counseling or examining our relationship because you didn't do that in the churches we hailed from. Then suddenly, after twenty-eight years of marriage, we joined a new church, and suddenly we met Gary, our marriage counselor, and light dawned in the swamp of my heart. And with the dawning, I discovered I'd been a disrespectful nag, a whiner with a victim mentality, someone with enough spiritual baggage to crush a pack mule into a greasy oil stain. I was a spiritual mess, and had been one for all my adult years and never realized it.

I still remember the day I realized what a mess of a wife I'd been. It was a glorious, freeing, agonizing realization as I fled into the arms of Jesus. As I turned to Him in sorrow for my sin, I felt His love surround me as I'd never felt it before. In many ways, His voice became real to me for the first time in that moment. My life and Dan's and our marriage have never been the same.

But how had I been so blind for so long to the person I'd been? For years I'd never heard my own self-deceptions. But once I began to listen, I began to see the true nature of the monster of self-talk that wielded control over my thoughts, attitudes, and actions.

THE TRUTH BEHIND THE TRUTH

Our counselor Gary helped me look at my battles and ask questions that helped me see what I was actually telling myself, then to evaluate my motives and goals. I learned to pull back from my thoughts, then ask, "What are you saying? Is it really true?" Once I'd answered those questions, I forced myself back to the same questions a second time: "What's the truth behind the truth? What are you *really* telling yourself?" As I studied my self-talk, I discovered that I often lied to myself or diminished the truth. It could take question after question and long periods of prayer and self-reflection for me to get at the core of my motives.

I was making progress, finding motives hidden beneath the excuses I'd made for so many years. Then a few months ago God decided to give me a vivid example of how easy it is for me to slip into rationalization and accusation to let myself off the hook.

WHEN SELF-TALK GOES BAD

With our counselor's help, Dan and I made commitments to changes in our marriage. I began examining my thoughts, attitudes, and compulsion to take control, while Dan worked on his pattern of passivity. We were making progress and experiencing greater trust in our communication. Then one afternoon I decided to ask Dan about a balance on a debt. We'd been working to pay it off, but I was suspicious the balance might be higher than I'd hoped. In typical style, I threw discretion out the window and asked about it at our anniversary dinner at a nearby restaurant.

I felt my anger stirring even before I formed my first question. I knew it was likely I was going to get an answer I didn't like. But for once I explored the motives for my anger and began to listen to my self-talk as I felt the tension mounting inside of me.

So what's your motive for having this conversation in the first place?

To get information about our credit card balance.

Really? Then you only want information and it won't matter what Dan's answer will be?

Of course it will matter what his answer will be. I'm going to be ticked if the balance is a bazillion dollars. Or anything more than the number I've already decided in my head.

Well you could have gotten the balance from paperwork at home. So what's really your motive?

I have a right to get mad if he's messed this up. This is about his leadership and stewardship of our money. He should be thinking about HIS motives so I wouldn't have to be thinking about mine.

You're avoiding the question, which was, What's your motive for having this conversation, on your anniversary, in a public restaurant? I believe the focus of evaluating self-talk is supposed to be to look at the self who is talking.

> This is crazy. It's like having my counselor in my head 24/7. Okay, then. My motive is to open up the lines of conversation about something important in our marriage.

Can you do that here and now and do it well?

> I don't know.

Really? I think you do know. Is it better to have that conversation here and now or better to wait?

> I hate waiting. I don't want to wait.

Yes. That's always been a problem, hasn't it?

At this point Dan broke into the silence and asked me why I was being so quiet. I'm sure he was fearful, as quietness on my part usually indicated I was slipping into a migraine or preparing for a verbal onslaught.

"I'm thinking before I speak and trying to do something right for once," I answered. He raised an eyebrow. I thought for a moment he might choke on his coffee. Shelly pondering before she spoke!

> But I want to talk about it right now.

Why?

> Because I will explode if I don't, and we need to communicate about this. And if I make myself talk about it here, it will help me be calm and in control. I can do this right for once if I make up my mind.

I forced myself to inhale three times as I chose my words, then asked for the balance. I was stunned to hear an amount twice what I'd hoped to hear. A succession of sarcastic questions flew into my brain, but I forced myself to silently evaluate them.

Why is your first response sarcasm?

> To make him feel bad and make myself feel better at his expense.

Then figure out a way to say something that won't attack him.

This infuriates me. I'm too mad to stay and eat dinner. I'm going to walk home.

And why do you want to walk out?

Because it feels good. Because I'm too mad to talk. Because I need to cool off.

Why don't you stay here and cool off? Take a sip of water. Chew on a chimichanga. But give this to God. Take the conversation in a positive direction.

I can't.

You won't. If you sit here long enough swirling your straw in that glass, you'll think of something that isn't sarcastic or an attack. Why don't you ask him why he didn't tell you about the balance? Think about your tone, your body language.

Can't I even punish him with that?

No.

A long silence hung between Dan and me as the argument raged in my head, and I toyed with the idea of whether or not to bolt for the door. He watched me with one eyebrow raised. He recognized a woman doing battle and knew my commitment to break free from my patterns of verbal attack and blame. I sat silently as I fought the desire to walk out the door, to cross my arms and sling icy daggers with my eyes. Instead, I focused on my thoughts, on my steady stream of excuses and lies, until a right response finally settled in my heart. Not a perfect response, but one not dripping with accusation and blame. A response I could articulate in an even tone and with an honest expression.

"You kept this to yourself and never told me. Why?"

His answer came quickly. "I was afraid you'd be angry. I knew whenever or however I told you, it would be my fault. I feel rotten about this. We both hate debt and know emergencies got us here."

My tears had shifted into free flow. Dan hadn't told me because he knew he could count on the response of an angry, punishing wife.

An embarrassed waiter hovered in my peripheral vision, and I waved him over. Dan and I ordered, then talked over a simple plan for paying down the balance before setting the topic aside for discussion later.

Even though Dan and I had been married for thirty-two years, it was a first anniversary for me—the first where I confronted and defeated the monster of self-talk. And the first where I recognized I could break patterns that had held me captive for years and walk into the life God had envisioned for me.

THE MONSTER THAT LIES BENEATH

Many of our thoughts are conscious, and we're aware of their implications on our attitudes and actions. But others play out on a level that lies below the surface of our awareness. The science that lies behind lie detectors, for instance, demonstrates that our body produces physiological changes in heart rate and breathing in response to our thoughts. Even the most hardened criminal would be challenged by the science of outthinking a lie detector. Our bodies are designed to respond at the cellular level to the stress of telling ourselves lies.

For instance, we're usually aware of our thought processes during a debate or argument as we choose our words, shape our case, and select the perfect word as we attempt to outmaneuver our spouse or teenager. But what about those days when we're driving to work engrossed in plans and that *How did I get here?* feeling sweeps over us? We evaluated our surroundings, changed lanes, braked, and accelerated, all acts that required thought but that we carried on at a subconscious level of awareness. Similarly, a rolling subscript of self-talk underscores everything we say and do as we cruise through daily life.

- We're irritated before the day even begins, and we chalk it up to "getting up on the wrong side of the bed."
- We nurse a spirit of irritation toward our boss and convince ourselves that the problem is his, not ours.
- We holler at the woman who cuts us off in traffic because there's nothing wrong with blowing off a little steam now and then.
- We repeat a little gossip, telling ourselves that we shared it out of a spirit of true concern for a friend.
- We turn our heads as the offering plate passes, as we mull over our frustration over the last decision made by someone in church leadership.

In most of these circumstances and others like them, we lie to ourselves about the truth. We often twist what God *really* said to suit our own desires. Seduced by Satan's voice, we place our hands over our ears and tune out God's voice of truth.

Satan's goal is to deafen us to God's voice so that we embrace his thinking as easily and naturally as if it were God's very own.

Did God really say . . .

Satan's words were just a suggestion, after all. An implication. A seed intended to stir us to sin. And the power of *really* rises up in all of us today—the desire for our thoughts to take precedence over God's. For our plans to subvert His. For our character to judge His. With those four words, Satan assassinated God's character in the garden. He subverted trust, and he set mankind on a path of independent thinking. With those four words, the monster of sin was conceived.

And it all began in the silence of self-talk.

ADMITTING WE'RE LIARS

The day I learned my proposal for this book had been accepted, I poured myself a stiff drink of caffeine-free diet Coke, collapsed at the kitchen table with my head in my hands, and considered writing this book under the name of the girl in sixth grade who'd teased me for being fat. That way I pour out the slime of my life and get revenge all at the same time. Of course, this would pretty much pervert God's desires for me to love Him with all my heart and to love others as myself—even my childhood enemies. Writing the book would mean admitting the truth—in black and white. What was even worse was realizing I couldn't write a book about struggling with the lies in my head without wanting to lie about the lies in my head.

But I'm in good company. The apostle Paul tells us we all wrestle with sin, no matter how good our intentions.

> *I know that nothing good lives in me, that is, in my sinful nature. For I have the desire to do what is good, but I cannot carry it out. For what I do is not the good I want to do; no, the evil I do not want to do—this I keep on doing.*
>
> —Romans 7:18–19

As ugly and sinful as my heart can be, the Bible tells me we're all sinners down to the core of our twisted motives.

Jeremiah 17:9 puts it well: "The heart is deceitful above all things and beyond cure. Who can understand it?"

In the privacy of our thoughts, we rationalize bitterness and anger—toward spouses, family members, bosses and coworkers, toward those who abuse and persecute us, even those we love. We envision scenarios, conversations, rebuttals, quick comebacks. We quietly revel in their downfalls, judge their lives, and inwardly sneer at their pain.

We turn a blind eye toward those in need and justify our self-indulgence. We harden our hearts to a true spirit of generous giving and raise our voices in cries for more. We refuse to admit that everything we have is God's in the first place and wrap our arms around His good gifts as if they somehow belong to us.

The voice of the Father recedes into the background as our own rises and obscures the truth. And Satan's work is done. Seduced by deadly thoughts, we turn from God and all that was good to a barren life severed from the intimacy of His presence.

TIPPING YOUR EAR TOWARD YOUR SOUL

My life changed when I realized that my self-talk determines the quality of my love for God. The issues of my life spring from my mind. My thoughts determine how I love others. It determines how I treat people who disrespect me, who abuse me. It determines how I give and why I give. It determines who I value and why I value them. It determines how and why I clean my toilets, whether or not I give generously to God's church, my attitude toward the poor, the environment, missions, and how I pray. Most important, it determines who I believe I am and who I believe God is.

Satan's goal is to deflect our eyes from God and onto ourselves. And he wants us to be unaware of the literal battle in our hearts caused by the fall. He wants us to focus our eyes and our hearts on our needs, our desires, our rights. He is the enemy and wants to harden our hearts to God's love, without ever giving it a second thought.

He wants us to question God's loving, good intentions toward us and His holy, righteous character.

He wants us to question God's gift of redemption and providing a way back to Him when we mess up.

As children of God, we all stand shoulder to shoulder with Adam and Eve in their first sin, questioning God, doing battle with the voices that call us to become our own gods. If we stop and listen, we can hear the voice of seduction calling.

Do anger and bitterness chatter in your ear? Do your wounds say you have a right to a little payback?

Do the voices of envy and jealousy whisper in your thoughts—comparison, lust, frustration, dreams that have always eluded you?

What about dissatisfaction? You'll never measure up. Life is always letting you down. You're simply a victim, so why even try?

Is Satan speaking abandonment, rejection, criticism, and blame into your soul?

If you listen, you'll hear the hiss beneath the surface.

Then pray that God will give you discernment, wisdom, and a passion to conform your mind, will, and emotions to His will. He desires nothing more than to open the eyes of your heart and to draw you close to Him so you can learn to love Him with the abandon of His child in the garden—with all your heart, soul, and strength.

SOUL SEARCH
Breaking the Silence

- In what areas of your life or what times of your life have you struggled with a sense of entitlement? What has your self-talk sounded like, and how has it influenced your choices and your daily life?
- Can you recall any conversations similar to Shelly's in the restaurant? Were there actual dueling opinions in your mind? How did your situation play out?
- Where do you believe your greatest battles lie in the struggle for truth in your life? Can you describe how your self-talk influences you?
- How do you approach these battles when they occur? What two simple steps could you take to be more proactive in heightening your awareness of ungodly self-talk and replacing it with God's truth?

FACING THE SEDUCTION
Listening to the Spirit and the Word

Read Jean's letter below.

a. What voices—what lies—do you think she was listening to, and how do you think they may have drowned out God's voice in her life?

Have you ever struggled with similar lies and why?

b. As a friend, how would you have responded to Jean in her situation? Why?
c. How does a sense of entitlement play into our thoughts when our loved ones have been maliciously harmed? How does this balance with biblical justice?

I KNEW THE BIBLE TOLD ME to love my enemies. I'd heard it preached all my life and even thought I was doing it. I was never a person who lost my temper much, but I guess I thought I was a lot more spiritual than people who did. But no one had ever really done anything terrible to me until a family friend sexually molested my daughter. Suddenly, I had all kinds of hatred running circles in my head.

I told myself I had a right to be outraged at what he'd done to my little girl. Rage quickly turned into rehearsals of how I wanted him to suffer—not just pay for what he'd done, but have horrible, evil things happen to him. I'd practiced this way of thinking all my life but on a smaller scale. Someone elbowed me out of a job once, and every time I heard about their struggles or disappointments after that, I secretly gloated. I told myself it was what they deserved. For a long time I told myself the man who'd laid hands on my child deserved stoning. Didn't the Old Testament teach capital punishment for these kinds of things?

I told myself I was entitled to despise him, and I refused to admit I was feeding my bitterness. I knew the Bible told me to love my enemies and pray for people who acted spitefully. I just found ways to deceive myself into thinking that those parts of the Bible didn't apply to me because, more than anything, I wanted to hang on to what I thought was my right to hate the man who'd hurt my daughter so badly.

—Jean B.

RESPONDING FROM THE HEART
Prayer

Dear Heavenly Father, Day after day I'm locked in battles to believe what suits my life, and Satan would like me to be oblivious to the fact that I lie to myself about what I think I'm due. Forgive me for turning away from You and Your truth in the sin of entitlement that pollutes so much of my thinking. Open my eyes to the fact that I choose lies over truth. Help me to hear my self-talk from Your perspective so I can arm myself with Your wisdom and Your truth. My greatest desire is to love You with all my heart, soul, and mind and to love people out of my overflow of love for You.

Help me to be still and listen, Lord. May I be slow to speak so that I can begin to evaluate what's in my heart—what I'm thinking and want to say and why I want to say it. Help me begin to see my twisted motives and goals and to give them to You. My desire is to be a child again in the garden, loving You passionately and walking in the freedom of the person You created me to be. Amen.

CHAPTER 3

Lessons *from a Dead Man on a Pole:*

How the Life We Think We See Shapes the Lies We Believe

The heart has eyes which the brain knows nothing of.

—Charles H. Perkhurst

WHEN EXPECTATIONS THROW YOU OFF COURSE

The family history trip of 1985 was my husband Dan's idea. My adult children still shudder when we refer to it.

It was a trip that proved that Dan and I define the terms "vacation fun" differently. He thought our children would find it fun riding six hours a day without air conditioning in the backward-facing seat of our vintage station wagon, eyeball-to-eyeball with the driver of the car following us.

They did not.

He thought they would be enthralled to view museums, plaques, monuments, and people dressed in Civil War costumes.

They were not.

He thought it would be fun to stay in the homes of well-meaning and generous friends unfortunate enough to live near anything remotely historical—friends whose spare bedroom windows were painted shut in the sweltering heat of summer and who welcomed our children with gifts of illegal fireworks and jawbreakers the size of bowling balls that lodged in our children's armpits and had to be removed at roadside rest areas.

I did not.

And I have long believed that these dear and gracious friends prayed caller ID into existence, and every spring since God answered their prayers, they have checked all incoming numbers, muttering, "Don't pick it up if it's the Beaches. They're planning another cheap vacation."

But Dan had planned this trip, and I'd determined it was our sacred family duty to enjoy it, even if it made us crazy. For Nathan and Dan, the highlight of the trip was going to be a tour through the Baseball Hall of Fame in Cooperstown, New York. For Jessica, the highlight was going to be getting home. The highlight for me would be a tour through the Fennimore House and Art Museum, James Fennimore Cooper's early nineteenth-century farmhouse. (Trust me, no one was with me on this one.)

We'd been driving for several hours the morning we pulled into Cooperstown, and we were looking forward to a break. But I immediately became frustrated when I realized we'd become entangled in a traffic jam. Jessica and Nathan were in the back of the car complaining about the heat and starvation. Dan and I were exasperated and hoping for a break to escape whining kids, sticky seats, and each other.

As the traffic inched along, I noticed a huge turn-of-the-century building in front of us with emergency vehicles crowding the parking lot. The grounds were teeming with people staring toward the street, where ambulances, fire trucks, and police cars were gathered. By now the traffic was crawling so slowly that we would have made better time if we'd been walking. We were approximately a hundred feet from the emergency vehicles before I realized that the crowd was staring into the air, and my eyes followed theirs.

At the top of a utility pole, a workman hung limply from a safety belt. He was dressed in the uniform of a worker from the local power company, and he wore a yellow hard hat. Beneath him, emergency workers were trying to extricate him from the power source. A fireman was slowly climbing the pole, harness in hand, to retrieve the worker as EMTs and paramedics stood ready below. He calculated each handhold and foothold with the steady gaze of a surgeon as a man in a hard hat coached him from below.

The crowd stood below in silence and looked on. Dan and I felt our chests tighten as the reality of the scene set in.

Tragedy was playing out in front of our eyes. We tried to turn away, but we couldn't.

NEW VISION, NEW REALITY

Nothing could ever erase the horror of that moment.

Jessica and Nathan's voices faded, along with my concerns about our broken air conditioner, hunger, and bickering children.

A memory flooded through me—the sound of a thud, then a moan, as I'd scrambled upstairs to our children's bedrooms and found Nathan semiconscious in his room, electrocuted through the mouth. He'd attempted to chew through an electrical cord. My child, not even two, had lain lifeless in my arms.

The man on the pole was someone's child.

A wave of nausea washed over me, and I turned toward the backseat and drank in the face of my son, his face pressed against the glass as he stared silently at the scene beyond the window. The scars of the plastic surgery on his lips were barely visible. Next to him, Jessica craned her neck to look through his window.

We all watched in horror. It was impossible to tell whether the man was simply unconscious or actually dead. It took three or four minutes for our car to pass as the worker at the top of the pole worked deftly to assess the man's condition, then began the work of bringing him down. It felt like an hour, but we couldn't force our eyes away until at last the scene faded from view and Dan turned and headed randomly in another direction.

Thoughts of the Baseball Hall of Fame and Fennimore House diminished. We drove around Cooperstown in stunned silence. No one was hungry but we knew we had to give the kids a chance to eat before we headed to our next destination.

We chose a local diner, and I scanned people's faces and even eavesdropped for information, but no one seemed to be discussing the accident. But I wasn't dissuaded. I had to know whether or not the man had lived. If there was hope, I wanted to share it with my children. So I approached the cashier and explained that my husband and our family were tourists and what we'd witnessed down the street.

I'd steeled myself for every possible reaction, but I wasn't prepared for the cashier's stunning response.

She laughed.

"That was a community disaster drill, honey. That man wasn't hurt a lick. He'll probably be in later with his family giving us all the details."

THE MAGIC EYE

Suddenly, everything I thought I'd seen so clearly morphed into a new image of reality, like a Magic Eye poster that pops into three-dimension clarity. What I'd believed to be true was untrue. I'd seen an accurate, detailed picture, but I'd been deceived into thinking something false about what my eyes had taken in.

I'd been deceived because I'd seen only circumstances, but circumstances weren't the whole picture. The truth was, I'd viewed the man on a pole from a limited perspective. But seeming tragedy turned to joy when our perspective changed and someone who knew the whole story told us the truth.

Finding out the truth lifted a cloud and restored our joy. Our conversation resumed. Our countenances changed. Our appetites returned. We let the kids order dessert, and we left a huge tip.

LESSONS FROM THE DEAD MAN

I'd looked at the circumstances before me that day and believed what my eyes and ears told me to believe. The facts seemed to be clear enough. Really, if I couldn't believe what my own eyes and ears told me, what could I believe?

My mind filled in a few spaces as I read between the lines of what I'd seen, all the while blind to the truth that God's sovereignty sustains us between the lines. His grace undergirds us between the lines. His sufficiency surrounds us between the lines. His wisdom defines us between the lines. Apart from Him, what I see is only a mirage produced by the shimmers of death rising from this dead and rotting world. I'd slipped into the mind-set of the curse of sin—believing I could interpret my world from my limited perspective. I didn't see that true perspective encompasses the entire context of life and the purpose, objectives, roles of each individual in history. Someone, somewhere, had gone to a great deal of trouble to plan every detail of a safety drill for the welfare of Cooperstown. And from my limited perspective, I'd quickly judged it all to be a tragedy.

The moment Satan whispered his first words of doubt to Eve, she should have hollered for her Maker. She knew who was in charge, and she knew Him intimately. He'd formed her flesh, shaped the curve of her breasts and the slope of her shoulders, and He'd stamped His image in her spirit. He'd dreamed a dream for her future and set it into motion in a place of perfect beauty, security, and promise.

Every cell of Eve's body should have been quivering with gratitude for all she'd been given—especially for the gift of an intimate relationship with God Himself. The dust of Mars should have reverberated with the sound of her praise. She'd been given perfection, peace, paradise, and yet as Satan questioned God's good intentions for her, gratitude didn't spring from her lips.

A few years back, dear friends of ours took Dan and me on an all-expenses-paid cruise through the Panama Canal. When we learned we were going, you couldn't shut me up. I was overwhelmed by generosity too big for my brain. For the next few years, every friend, neighbor, and relative who came within ten feet of me heard not only the details of our trip, but how grateful we were to have been so indulged. I'm sure more than a few people wanted to shove a cork in my mouth.

God always knew that Eve would listen to the serpent and doubt Him, so He certainly wasn't surprised by what happened in the garden of Eden. Yet we can learn from Eve's sin. Imagine how the drama might have played out if Eve had spouted thanks like hot lava the day Satan approached her. What if her thoughts had been so full of praise for God's goodness that Satan's questions couldn't have found a foothold?

Satan: "Did God really say . . ."

Eve: "Are you talking about *my* God? Have I told you what He did for me just this morning? Get a whiff of that honeysuckle right in front of you. Have you ever smelled anything so divine? Every day when I get up I discover something new He's created just for me. Have I told you how wonderful He is? But hold on—you were asking a question, and I'd rather you heard the answer straight from Him. If I ask, He'll be here beside me faster than you can say 'Snake-in-the grass.'"

(Sounds of slithering as serpent makes a hasty exit.)

CLOUDED GLASS

Like Eve, I chat every day with the serpent and never think to holler out to my Creator. I look at life behind the rolled-up window of my car, thinking I know it all, passing judgment on God, others, and the world. I fail to recognize that I see life superficially, that my perspective is temporal, rather than eternal, and that of the created and not the Creator. I don't know the beginning or the end of my story or the stories of those around me. I can't draw a single breath on my own, and neither can the world's greatest doctors or scientists. I can blink my eyes, but I don't understand how I do it. I can play the piano, but I don't control how my eyes, muscles, and brain coordinate to move my fingers.

In both spiritual and earthly matters, I'm a child. I don't grasp the eternal context of life. First Corinthians 13:12 explains it: "Now we see but a poor reflection as in a mirror; then we shall see face to face. Now I know in part; then I shall know fully, even as I am fully known." Right now we can't fully trust what we see. We have limited knowledge. Only God sees our world from the top down, the bottom up, and the inside out.

I don't know why my dear friend and goddaughter Alicia had to endure forty brain surgeries before the age of eight. I don't know why her sister Stacy lived for only a few short days. I don't know why many of my friends are suffering with brutal forms of cancer. I don't know why tsunamis, earthquakes, floods, famine, disease, war, and persecution ravage our world every day.

But I do know that every day Satan whispers to me—"Does God *really* . . . "

Love you?

Look out for your best interests?

Control this chaotic world or care what happens in it?

The world we live in is filled with dead men. They stare back at us on the evening news and from the streets of our cities and small towns. They sip coffee with us, sit beside us at soccer games, shoot e-mails our way, share our sidewalks and our beds. We see their lifeless faces, their despair. At times they are our own.

In the empty spaces of doubt and apathy, a voice whispers that God is not in the garden. That He does not see us. That He does not care. That we are alone and abandoned. Doubt invades our soul.

God is not good. We're on our own.

THE SECRET OF A HEAVENLY PERSPECTIVE

Cooperstown residents who watched the emergency drill recognized that two levels of reality existed—what they were watching (a horrible scene) and the underlying reality (it was a drill). What they saw bolstered their sense of security and preparedness for their future. Most of them were probably glad they lived in a town where people were preparing citizens for what might lie ahead.

Once our hearts lose sight of our all-loving, all-knowing, all-powerful, holy God and the enormity of His compassion and redemptive work on our behalf, our thoughts plummet inward in a cascade of self-centeredness. Our vision of God's goodness and love wither, and gratitude dies. Our thoughts spiral downward into the abyss of self, as praise and thankfulness are torn from our lips. Our hearts become deaf to our Father's voice, and we lose sight of the dreams He dreamed for us, His plans for our lives.

We can only assume what passed through Eve's mind as she chatted with the serpent in the garden. But we know that the first words out of her mouth when Satan questioned God's intentions toward her weren't praise for all God had done for her or a defense of His character and good gifts.

Sound familiar?

Romans 1:20–21 describes our ingratitude:

> *For since the creation of the world God's invisible qualities—his eternal power and divine nature—have been clearly seen, being understood from what has been made, so that men are without excuse. For although they knew God, they neither glorified him as God nor gave thanks to him, but their thinking became futile and their foolish hearts were darkened.*

Only when we trade our earthbound perspective for God's heavenly, eternal perspective can we experience gratitude in the "dead man" moments of life. Our ability to praise in the tough times rests in acknowledging that our perspective on life is limited. We only see part of the story, but God sees it all and promises to work out everything for our good, in spite of the pain of this life. He will redeem our pain and bring purpose from even the most agonizing events of our lives. Because of this, we can look with confidence beyond what we see in this world to what lies ahead—the promise of heaven and our final redemption.

DEAD MEN AND THE POWER OF SELF-TALK

We live life based on perceptions. What we think we see shapes our attitudes, actions, and emotions. The sight of a man hanging, lifeless, from the top of a utility pole that summer day obliterated my sense of joy and expectation. It deadened my desires and appetite. It silenced my voice. I lost focus on what I'd come to Cooperstown to do.

I was unaware that I was forming perceptions through my self-talk, even as thoughts were taking shape. I envisioned a grieving widow and shattered children. And a memory clawed at my heart—holding my son, Nathan, to my chest after he'd been electrocuted through the mouth. As Dan and I drove through the streets of Cooperstown, I could still remember the weight of my baby's limp body in my arms as I'd held him on our excruciating ride to the hospital.

Images, perceptions, emotions flashed through my thoughts at 1,300 words per minute, and I never thought to question whether they were based on truth. But I did the only thing I knew how to do.

I prayed.

LINEBACKER MOMENTS

The truth struck me like an NFL linebacker when I discovered everything I'd believed had been based on my misinterpretation of circumstances. Unfortunately, I've had far too many linebacker moments in my life. The ten dollar term for those linebacker moments is *paradigm shift*.

Just months before Dan and I were married, I was assaulted by a rapist who'd raped over forty women over the course of several summers. The night he attacked me, he had raped a woman in her seventies, as well as a fourteen-year-old girl. A police officer later told me that this man was the most notorious sex offender in Michigan at the time.

I spent several years of my life hating this man. Voices inside my head whispered, accused, and raged. One argued that I'd drawn a line down the center of my soul, like a sibling slapping a crayon line down the middle of a shared bedroom. I hated the man I considered my mortal enemy, and I enjoyed hating him, yet I knew the Bible told me to love him. I nursed my grudge and fed it while I spouted verses, sang hymns, and did my devotions.

And I was an equal-opportunity dispenser of hatred. I hated the lawyer who'd defended him seven times for rape and gotten him off on technicalities. I hated the judicial system that allowed rapists to walk free to rape again. I hated myself for allowing him to see me on the porch that night and know I was home. I hated . . . and I hated . . . and I hated. And all the while I was unaware that the voice of the Holy Spirit was speaking to me from one side of the crayon line while lies raged from the other side.

Then one day a pastor's simple sermon flattened me with a linebacker moment. As he preached the Word, I suddenly heard the lies for what they were. Conversations with myself began to bubble to the surface of my thoughts as I saw the hatred I'd harbored.

I'd been seduced by sin and been deceived.

In one powerful paradigm shift, I saw my evil motives and horrible pride. I'd believed I was so much better than the man who'd attacked me. I'd reveled in hate, my own silent, self-justified perversion. I'd wanted him to go to hell while wallowing in self-righteousness.

In one stunning second, I was body-slammed to the ground at the sight of my sin.

The self-talk that had been running through my head had come straight from the pit of hell itself, and I had nursed my sinful motives like a mother feeds her child. My sin of hate had perverted God's desire for me to pour His love into the world, and my sin of hate was as heinous as my molester's sin of rape. The Word of God helped me see the great divide that split my heart. In one flash of truth, I saw myself with new eyes, and I saw the man who'd molested me with new eyes. My thinking was transformed.

He was a sinner, just like me, a man God loved and asked me to learn to love and forgive.

For the first time, I could see myself standing side by side at the foot of the cross with the man I'd once hated.

LIVING ABOVE THE CRAYON LINE

Galatians 2:20 tells us, "I have been crucified with Christ and I no longer live, but Christ lives in me. The life I live in the body, I live by faith in the Son of God, who loved me and gave himself for me." Crucifying means that I take captive my thought life. I become a student of what I think—of my attitudes, my motives, my tendencies to fall into my legacy of ingratitude and selfishness.

God wants to conform us to the image of His Son, Jesus Christ.

In order to crucify, I must first be a student of Scripture. I must search the Word of God to know truth and to claim it. I must be committed to prayer and to using the Bible to reveal my crooked thinking. I must pray specifically about what needs to be put to death in my thought life—pride, envy, a manipulative spirit, a compulsion for control, anger, greed, lying, lust, fear, lack of compassion, lack of generosity, and other sins or controlling elements.

Secondly, crucifying self requires submitting my will to God's. Too often we justify our attitudes and actions by telling ourselves that God wants us to be happy instead of holy. First and foremost, God wants to conform us to the image of His Son, Jesus Christ. Conformity is hard work because it requires consistency and a lifestyle of repentance and faith, in even the most difficult circumstances.

As I was learning to listen to my self-talk and my motives, I decided to focus on one simple task—trying to love a friend of mine according to the double love command of Matthew 22:37–39—with all my heart, soul, and mind. But there was one catch. She was the kind of friend who I usually had to grit my teeth to be around—abrasive and unkind to others. But I asked God to give me wisdom to love her as I'd want to be loved. Who'd have thought something so simple could be so hard?

I began by paying attention to my self-talk, forcing myself to stop and listen to what I wanted to say before I said it. I evaluated my thought processes throughout the day, asking myself what it would really mean to speak in love, to act in love, to be motivated by love, paying special attention to what prompted my words and actions in my friend's presence.

Before the end of the first day, I didn't like what I was seeing about myself. Self-protective motives were prompting me to say and do self-protective things. Judgmental thoughts and arrogant comparisons were drifting through my mind. When I tried to be kind, I found my motives were often self-serving. When I prayed for my friend, I prayed shallow prayers that she would somehow be changed, but I discovered that I didn't want to be involved in her journey because it might cost me, relationally or emotionally.

My decision to love someone transformed into a painful exercise in self-discovery. As I pulled myself away from thoughts and "hovered above the crayon line" in my soul, I began to see things about myself that exposed my hidden motives, but it was in those moments that God could begin forming new motives in me.

Truth rests in the character of God and in His Word. They stand as our judge and jury in all things. Until we lift our eyes away from details and circumstances, we will never see eternal truth from a heavenly perspective. Satan will always try to distract us, lure us with promises of power to become our own gods, and tempt us to question God's love for us and His delight in our highest good.

Did God really say . . .

Tip your ear toward your soul and listen. Turn up the volume. The echo of those words from the garden cling to your motives. Allow the Spirit of God to focus His revealing power on your heart. Then wait with an open spirit, prepared to learn and to receive.

The Father is calling you to the hopes, dreams, and plans He's envisioned for you from the foundations of the earth—to His true legacy as His child.

SOUL SEARCH

Breaking the Silence

- Relate a time when you've had a limited perspective on a circumstance that resulted in wrong messages playing in your head. How was truth eventually revealed, or was it? How did you handle the situation? Were people wounded as a result of your actions and words, based on your self-talk?
- Read Romans 1:20–21. What roles do gratitude and ingratitude play in your self-talk and your behavior? Give at least one example from your day-to-day living.
- Step back from the "crayon line" in your soul. What aspects of anger are you holding on to? What twinges of jealousy creep into your thinking? What control issues are you struggling with? What things has God nudged you to put down that you pick up? What sinful attitudes do you justify? What steps can you take to help you listen for God's voice of truth? Refer to appendix 8 for suggestions for journaling your self-talk and learning how to evaluate self-centered, entitled motives.

- Imagine yourself in Shelly's situation with her sexual assault or perhaps a painful circumstance when you were victimized. How did pride and anger influence your inner dialogues? What attitudes did you tell yourself you had a right to? What conversations have played out in your head, and how did they keep you from passionately following God's truth? Are you still struggling?

FACING THE SEDUCTION
Listening to the Spirit and the Word

Read Pat's letter below, then answer the following questions:

a. What inner voices do you think widows are particularly susceptible to falling prey to hearing?
b. What do the following passages tell us about God's regard for widows and His concern for their welfare: Exodus 22:22; Deuteronomy 10:18; Psalm 146:9; Psalm 68:5.
c. How were the Word of God, the Spirit of God, and the people of God implemented in a three-pronged attack on Pat's negative voices?
d. What specific truth from the Word of God do you see evidenced in Pat's letter—truth that helped her defeat Satan's lies?
e. How has Pat's life been different since she confronted her self-talk and the voices in her heart?

WHEN MY HUSBAND passed away a few years ago, my first thought was that I wasn't smart enough to be a widow. The fears that played out in my mind caused me to stay away from church because I was afraid to do anything alone. I'd come from humble beginnings and hadn't become one of God's children until I was forty years old. My inner voices loved to tell me, "Pat, you're too old, too out of touch. You don't look good enough. You're not smart enough." I used to believe those words.

But now I know where to go to quiet those inner voices—right to God's Word. God's dealt with all those insecurities, and He's helped me see the lovable Pat, the Pat He designed, the Pat He knew before she was even born. He made me to be just the way I am, so

I'd better appreciate His handiwork.

I've always been surrounded by people who love and care about me. Those are the people God has used to make me able to be alone and happy. God's hand of protection in my life came in the form of two women who ministered to widows in our church. They gently drew me back into a social life where I could spend time with other women who'd experienced similar loss. Through Bible study, I met women who were different from me but who had their own struggles in life.

God has absolutely blessed my widowhood by placing me among godly people and giving me the time and the tools to "bloom"—no longer as a wife and helpmate to my husband, but as an independent person who is alone, but capable and content. Through the people in my church, the Lord has taught me, changed me, stretched me, and challenged me to do things I never thought I was capable of doing.

I still hear inner voices, but I only listen to those whispered by the Holy Spirit, who speaks to me deep in my soul, telling me I'm valuable to Him.

—Pat F.

RESPONDING FROM THE HEART

Prayer

Dear Father, Your hands formed me, and Your fingerprints are on every inch of me. My every breath is sustained by You, and every thought I think is produced because of the wonders of Your creation.

Forgive me for not being overwhelmed with gratitude for all You've done for me, Father. I desire to have a heart that grows more passionate each day—a heart that cries out how wonderful You are, even when everything around me looks like chaos. I want to grow more passionately in love with You and to have a spirit of gratitude that erupts from my soul. Help me to grow an insatiable desire to think Your thoughts, speak Your words, and walk in the legacy You envisioned for me before the foundations of the earth—to be conformed to the image of Your Son, Jesus Christ. Amen.

CHAPTER 4

The DANCE of Doubt:

The Legacy Conceived in Genesis 3

We're not necessarily doubting that God will do the best for us; we are wondering how painful the best will turn out to be.

—C. S. Lewis

Imagine for a moment that your doctor finds a quarter-sized tumor in your lungs and a few other masses in your liver and spleen thrown in for good measure. With a smile and a handshake, he assures you they're totally benign. No tests or biopsies will be necessary. The tumors won't affect your future in any way.

Just trust him.

Or imagine you're a hundred miles from home in your minivan on your family vacation and your eight-year-old assures you he blew out a candle he'd lit in your bedroom just before you pulled away. Relax, not to worry. He's promised you he blew it out. He's eight, after all. Sit back and enjoy the ride.

Just trust him.

Think for a moment about the reality of how doubt affects your life each and every day—how it robs you of sleep, of joy, of certainty, of hope. If only we lived in a world where we could totally rely on the people around us, on our environment, on the circumstances of life.

We can't begin to comprehend the serenity of life in a world like that. It would be perfect. It would be Paradise. And we had it once.

Until a conversation in the garden that unleashed the power of war, rape, embezzlement, slavery, and every other sin, perversion, and degradation known to man.

A conversation that began with doubt, then moved to lies and the subtle seduction that hung in the silent spaces between the serpent's words.

GAGGING, OPPOSING, OUTWITTING GOD

Imagine a love so great that it poured out its creative forces to birth an entire universe on our behalf. Imagine the magnitude of a love that shaped the curve of a rose petal, selected the hue of a sunset, or designed the scallop of a butterfly wing for our pleasure and delight.

When we look at the beauty of creation, we should take it personally. God placed us here on earth in the center of a three-dimensional, living, breathing valentine that shouts His love for us. The beauty of creation is inescapable—we need only open our eyes or pause to listen in a meadow. The beauty of creation is possible because of God's inherent beauty. Beauty is rooted in Him and calls us to Him. Our very love of beauty draws us to a God who is the essence and originator of beauty. And the beauty we see around us is not only a reflection of who God is, but an expression of a love so immense that sunsets and seascapes are mere glimmers.

Our God provided everything we'd ever need. He didn't drop us on the doorstep of creation with a few groceries to get us by, then drive off to tend to bigger and better matters. He invited us to join Him in caring for His world. He presented us the keys to all He had and gave us the honor of tending and nurturing His amazing wonders. He sculpted our bodies, breathed His breath into us, set us on our feet, then gave us volition and stepped back.

He only asked that we love and trust Him in return.

Then with diabolical foresight and a few well-chosen words, Satan began his own work of creation—envisioning a false god—a perversion of the true, righteous, and holy God. The idol of selfishness was born, shrouded behind false motives and hidden agendas.

Genesis 3:1 introduces the serpent, the Father of Lies, the opposer and subverter of the true and holy God, as he sows seeds of doubt in Eve's heart, seeds that forever change the course of history and the nature of humanity.

> *Did God really say, "You must not eat from any tree in the garden"?*
>
> —GENESIS 3:1

Did God really say?

With those words, the destiny of mankind hung suspended as the dance of doubt began in Eve's mind.

Both the King James and New American Standard versions reflect that the first word spoken by the serpent in Genesis suggests previous words or an interrupted dialogue, perhaps a conversation Eve had been having with herself and the serpent grasped on to.[2]

***Yea**, hath God said* . . . Genesis 3:1 (KJV)
***Indeed**, has God said* . . . Genesis 3:1 (NASB)

Interestingly, Eve doesn't seem surprised to be chewing the fat with the serpent. His first word indicates he's either breaking into her thoughts or we're picking up a conversation somewhere in the middle. Perhaps she's met him before and he's gained her trust in previous chats. We really don't know. What we do know is that God had shown Himself to Adam and Eve through His creation, words, gifts, presence, touch, and His power, and she should *really* have had an indisputable vision of His character. But the serpent's words hung suspended in her thoughts as her thoughts flickered.

Did God really say?

With Satan's simple words, faith in the goodness and character of God was annihilated, and doubt and sin were birthed in the hearts of mankind. From that moment on, our minds became the battleground for a cacophony of voices—Satan's voice in its many disguises, the voice of the Spirit of God, and our voice, tainted by doubt in the character and pure intentions of our heavenly Father.

We gag the voice of God when we believe His intentions aren't good, His character is less than irreproachable, and that He can't be trusted. It happens in the split-second of time when our growing pangs of doubt override His voice.

And more often than not, we never feel a thing.

With Satan's second interchange with Eve, he speaks history's first blatant lie into existence.

> *"You will not surely die," the serpent said to the woman.*
>
> —Genesis 3:4

Imagine what Eve's reaction might have been. She'd never heard a lie before, and this first one was a jaw-dropper—assaulting the character of God and insinuating He hadn't spoken the truth. At the moment the words were spoken, Eve was faced with a choice regarding how she'd respond.

> *But you must not eat from the tree of the knowledge of good and evil, for when you eat of it you will surely die.*
>
> —Genesis 2:17

She was responsible for recognizing Satan's diabolical sleight-of-hand and responding to his distortions. You can almost hear the scorn in his tone.

"Not to worry. What's death anyway? Has any creature or creation in the garden ever experienced death? And you, Eve? Surely *you're* not going to die."

Satan's monumental assault upon God's character is beyond our ability to comprehend. In October of 1987, eighteen-month-old Jessica McClure fell into a well in her aunt's backyard. It took rescue workers fifty-eight hours to free Jessica as they worked tirelessly to keep her from dying of hypothermia and falling farther down the hole.

Imagine that such a well exists in your backyard and that, as a parent, you've used every means within your power to warn your child of its dangers and to protect her. Then a stranger comes into your yard one day, knowing fully that death lies within that gaping hole. That stranger draws your child's face close to his own and whispers, "Don't listen to your mom or your dad, honey. Nothing will happen to you if you step into that hole. It wouldn't be there if they didn't expect you to play there."

Do you feel the white-hot anger rising within you, as your every intention for the good of your child is perverted for evil? Do you feel the scorching fires of hell in the tones of that whisper?

The lie of Satan in Genesis 3:4 is twofold: (1) God lies to His children and (2) there aren't any consequences to your behavior anyway. Make your choices. Live your life. Step into that hole and life will be better than you ever imagined.

The truth is, we were all seduced in the garden. Since the moment Adam and Eve made their choice, humankind has opposed God, dangling our feet over the open hole of death. And once we opposed Him, we took the next step in the progression of sin: to attempt to outwit Him and become His equals.

Genesis 3:5 continues with Satan's infusion of deception into the world.

> *For God knows that when you eat of it your eyes will be opened.*
>
> —Genesis 3:5a

With these words, Satan planted a new thought in Eve's mind: God knows something you don't know, and He doesn't want you to figure it out. He's withholding the good things from your life.

When we fall into this trap, we burn up brain cells devising ways to create better plans for our life than God's. Like Ananias and Saphira, we may think we've outwitted God and come up with an idea that will finally get us what we want. But they were wrong. Dead wrong.

Ananias and his wife agreed to try to deceive the church into believing they'd selflessly given their all in an offering. But the words "lied to the Holy Spirit" indicate that they tried to dupe God. They were so self-deceived that they didn't think God would see their selfish hearts or their manipulation of truth in their self-talk. They plowed ahead with their own plans as though God might have had a temporary lapse in omnipotence just this once. Read about them in Acts 5:3–5.

Gag God.
Oppose Him.
Outwit Him.
Do all this, and you will have what you ultimately desire: you'll equal God.

And aren't we just like them sometimes? Creating our own self-centered plans and justifying them, then deceiving ourselves into thinking God isn't aware of our selfish and twisted self-motives? Telling ourselves He doesn't hear the ridiculous things we say inside our heads?

The real problem is, we don't listen to what our self-talk sounds like from God's perspective.

Jonah thought heading to Tarshish was a better idea than following God's instructions to go to Nineveh. He thought he could outwit God, too. "Jonah ran away from the Lord and headed for Tarshish . . . where he found a ship. . . . After paying the fare, he went aboard and sailed for Tarshish to flee from the Lord" (Jonah 1:3). But God took care of Jonah's plans with the flick of a fin and one giant gulp.

Look around you at a world tangled in knots to outwit God. He's spelled out His plan clearly in His Word, but the world has rejected it and turned to every imaginable reinvention of the truth.

Sin's labor pains continue as the serpent and Eve carry on their dialogue. His purposes take root as he whispers his lies into her heart.

Gag God.

Oppose Him.

Outwit Him.

Do all this, and you will have what you ultimately desire: you'll equal God.

EQUALING GOD

As long as man has existed, he's sought knowledge that would make him equal to God. Whether displayed through the life of cult leaders, through humanity's fascination with astrology, or through the pages of bestselling books like Rhonda Byrne's *The Secret,* our desire to be gods and control our universe has always been with us—a desire birthed in the garden of Eden.

> *. . . and you will be like God, knowing good and evil.*
>
> —Genesis 3:5b

And you will be like God. You will have power over good and evil. You alone will be the arbiter of what is right and wrong for your life. But the "knowing of good and evil" that the serpent implied and the "knowing good and evil" that Eve experienced after the fall were two diabolically disparate things.

There is the knowledge of poverty a philanthropist has, who invests his or her resources into the eradication of poverty.

And there is the knowledge of poverty the homeless have,

knowledge that is visceral, that aches and burns, that knows hunger and suffering.

Satan's diabolical deception was to lure man to new knowledge—captivating, experiential knowledge that would result in pure and utter enslavement.

In one sense, mankind came to "know" evil in the exchange in the garden in a spiritually and historically transformational way.

> *Just as sin entered the world through one man, and death through sin, and in this way death came to all men, because all sinned.*
>
> —Romans 5:12

In one millisecond in history, evil became wed to Adam's and Eve's nature, indwelling all humans for the remainder of time. At the opening of Genesis chapter 3, Adam and Eve stood in the garden as pure image-bearers of their Maker, entrusted with all He'd created for their enjoyment, reflecting all that is true and pure, honorable and virtuous, just and righteous. Then in the moments it takes for doubt to take root, for selfishness and pride to be stirred, the world shuddered as the Lord's plan for eternity groaned under the weight of sin.

We're unable to comprehend the magnitude of the rift that occurred in that millisecond between God and mankind. But just a few short steps from the garden, in Genesis chapter 4, we see the fruit of the knowledge of good and evil—civilization crumbling as one brother's blood is spilled at the hands of another with Cain's murder of Abel.

Eve got her desire. Her sons became arbiters of their own truth as they fought to equal God.

And we follow in their footsteps as heirs to our birthright.

We hide our wedding ring in our pocket before we enter the hotel room.

We slander the object of our hate and justify our bitterness.

We degrade, disrespect, and dishonor others, forgetting whose image they bear.

We make petty plans and forget our purpose.

We elevate our intellect and disregard our Creator.

We live life for the moment, without regard to eternal consequences. Life becomes an exercise in self-centered futility, as we glut ourselves on the sensual, the material, and the temporal.

Satan slips from the garden and disappears, knowing we can be left to our own thoughts and our selfish desires.

BECOMING OUR OWN GODS

With four simple phrases, Satan sowed the seeds of sin that would produce every form of perversion and unrighteousness the world would ever know. In that moment as Eve stood face-to-face with the serpent, three voices fought for control of her mind, will, and emotions.

The voice of her Creator, the source of truth, who spoke truth into existence and into her life.

The voice of Eve's soul, as the woman God created her to be in intellect, emotions, spirit, and giftedness.

And the voice of the serpent, the Father of Lies, who lusted to pervert all that was true, righteous, just; his intent was to destroy what God had created and usurp His best intentions for His children.

Eve yielded to her thoughts. She chose what she thought was best for herself and became her own god.

> *When the woman saw that the fruit of the tree was good for food and pleasing to the eye, and also desirable for gaining wisdom, she took some and ate it. She also gave some to her husband, who was with her, and he ate it.*
>
> —Genesis 3:6

Reaching for the fruit was the visible evidence of Eve's sin. In an effort to satisfy her own desires, she placed herself on the throne of self-worship.

What should be terrifying to us is that Eve's rationale in verse 6 is one Christians often use when admitting our choices are in conflict with God's Word, the Bible. We convince ourselves our sinful actions will benefit our lives. We tell ourselves our choices will fulfill us, bring us blessing, or help us attain something great in life. Like Eve, we become seduced by our dreams. We refuse to believe Satan's plots could destroy us and strip us of every good thing the Father's ever given us, leaving us in spiritual poverty beyond anything we could comprehend.

Scripture doesn't tell us when Satan left the garden, but by verse 6, he's vanished from the scene, his goal accomplished. He knows he's won the battle, and has laid claim to Eve's thoughts. Knowing Satan's tactics, we can be certain he immediately launched phase two—his plan for terrorizing Eve's life with guilt for the choice she'd made. First Satan, the destroyer, tempts, then seeks to enslave us, and then bind us with guilt and remorse.

Once we've bought into his lies, the enslavement chain drags us farther down a path of wrong choices. Verse 6 tells us Eve shared the fruit with her husband, an outward sign of their mutual sin. All the elements were in place for the first-ever, wild-and-crazy family argument, followed by a lifetime of marital conflict. Eve immediately demonstrated an ability for self-justification. Adam had taken the fruit, and she hadn't put a slingshot to his head. Maybe later she even figured out a way to blame him for not stopping her, for not being there to help out when she needed him. Where had he been anyway? Why did it have to be her taking on the serpent in the first place? You'd think he could have stepped up to the plate when his wife really needed him.

We can only imagine. But what we do know is that the cycle of sin continued, as Adam blamed his choice on his wife.

PROCURING POWER

Once we walk away from God, life becomes a quest to navigate on our own, a quest for power. We enjoy knowing we're powerful and that we know powerful people. We enjoy thinking about power. Bragging about power, planning ways to gain greater power for ourselves or those we love. We overtake others through words, actions, manipulation, or affiliation. Lust for power destroys families, fuels tyranny, and engenders war.

Jesus rebuked the religious leaders of His day for their love of power.

> *Woe to you Pharisees, because you love the important seats in the synagogues and greetings in the marketplaces.*
>
> —Luke 11:43

The Pharisees' addiction to power and fake spirituality revolted Jesus. And we can feed into the same addiction, nursing self-righteous, judgmental, pride-filled attitudes. Power mongering is alive and well today in the form of factionalism, politicizing, and cliquishness. And wielding power is as much a part of some church cultures as communion.

In our jobs, we're told to strive for success. But we're also pulled into games of office politics.

In relationships, we struggle with urges to control others, to make them like us, to overpower them with our agendas. People who don't think, act, talk, or walk like we do can sometimes drive us crazy. We may even deceive ourselves into thinking that being more like us means being more spiritual.

Our problem is that we confuse the world's power with God's. Eve failed to recognize the simple truth that as God's precious daughter, she *already possessed* the power He'd given her.

Satan had nothing to offer her—nothing. He was spinning lies out of thin air. From the beginning, God empowered us as His sons and daughters.

> *His divine power has given us everything we need for life and godliness through our knowledge of him who called us by his own glory and goodness.*
>
> —2 PETER 1:3

The book of Ephesians instructs us to seek the power of God in order to fulfill His goals.

> *I pray that out of his glorious riches he may strengthen you with power through his Spirit in your inner being, so that Christ may dwell in your hearts through faith. And I pray that you, being rooted and established in love, may have power, together with all the saints, to grasp how wide and long and high and deep is the love of Christ, and to know this love that surpasses knowledge—that you may be filled to the measure of all the fullness of God.*
>
> —EPHESIANS 3:16–19

The life-changing power of Jesus is available to us through the Holy Spirit so we can be filled with God's full measure of blessing. This should drive our thirst for power.

SELF-PROTECTION

Our self-protective instincts began with Eve. Admittedly, sometimes those instincts work for our good. When a rapist pressed a metal object to my head when I was nineteen, I downshifted into self-protective behavior without a single thought. I fought, screamed, and, ultimately, ran for my life.

But often our self-protective instincts are motivated by desires to get our own way. When the serpent suggested God wasn't acting in Eve's best interests, she let the assault on God's character stir deeper motives.

> *When the woman saw that the fruit of the tree was good for food and pleasing to the eye, and also desirable for gaining wisdom, she took some and ate it. She also gave some to her husband, who was with her, and he ate it . . . and they realized they were naked; so they sewed fig leaves together and made coverings for themselves.*
>
> —Genesis 3:6–7

Suddenly, trust turned to doubt. Fellowship became fear, and Adam and Eve dreaded facing their Maker. In their shame, they covered up their newfound feelings of guilt with whatever they could get their hands on—fig leaves stitched together with a defensive attitude.

When they left the garden, they didn't go with just the leaves on their backs. They walked away with a burden of guilt, self-protection, and defensiveness that they passed on to future generations. Since that day, man has struggled with skepticism and self-protective, manipulative spirits as we seek to position ourselves to gain the best possible advantage in the world.

POSITIONING OURSELVES

Once the chains of enslavement slide into place, Adam and Eve went into hiding. Something had changed. The transparency they'd enjoyed in their relationship with God was gone. We can't be sure what they were thinking, but we can assume they chose to hide because they knew something was drastically wrong.

Their first instinct was to cover up and take man's first stab at religion by sewing. For the first time, we see God's children working to make themselves acceptable in God's eyes. From there, they invented the blame game.

Adam blamed Eve, Eve blamed the serpent, and in the process, blame-shifting was birthed in our DNA as surely as our need to eat or drink. So it's easy to understand why for years I could discern my friend's sweeping gaze as she sized people up and judged them, but it took years for me to see my reflection in her actions. Like Adam and Eve and all of us, I'm by nature a finger-pointer.

But when I discovered the gift of listening to my self-talk, I discovered more about myself than at first I wanted to know. Often my motives are good and prompted by a loving, serving heart. Other times they're driven by a desire for selfish gain. Most often they're mixed. For this reason, Scripture tells us to test our motives.

> *Test me, O Lord, and try me, examine my heart and my mind; for your love is ever before me, and I walk continually in your truth.*
>
> —Psalm 26:2–3

In order to discern our mixed motives, we must apply the truth of Scripture to our lives as the Holy Spirit corrects us, convicts us, and trains us in righteousness.

> *You have known the holy Scriptures, which are able to make you wise for salvation through faith in Christ Jesus. All Scripture is God-breathed and is useful for teaching, rebuking, correcting and training in righteousness, so that the man of God may be thoroughly equipped for every good work.*
>
> —2 Timothy 3:15–16

As I'm more fully equipped to walk in God's love and grace, I find myself running into the arms of the one who's given me everything, crying, "Abba, Father! You and You alone."

PROMOTING OURSELVES

The enslavement chain always pulls us down to a new level of sin. Once we grab power and begin protecting and positioning ourselves, we're forced to become self-promoters. And no one can promote their own agenda like someone who feels responsible for their own interests. We know where we want to go and how we need to get there. Even if we believe in humility, service, and spiritual values, self-promotion has a way of bubbling to the surface.

Who's going to make sure we get credit for our hard work when it's time for our next job evaluation? Career advancement doesn't just happen these days.

Who's going to be sure our kid doesn't sit on the bench all basketball season? If we don't stick up for our child, who will?

Who's going to make sure the new members of the congregation know what really happened in that pastoral staff decision three years ago? If someone doesn't provide some perspective, the whole mess could happen again.

In a society that thrives on spin doctors, publicists, lobbyists, and media hype, something deep within us tells us it's culturally correct, even desirable, to promote our agendas and shine a little light on our accomplishments.

But what about promoting our agendas over God's? Our values over His? Our plans over His? When Eve stepped away from God, she stepped into the abyss of self, and she lost herself there.

Scripture paints only a sketch of what happened in the garden, but it appears that Adam and Eve didn't give their decision great thought. The fruit would bring the fulfillment of their dreams. But as the sweet flesh hit their stomachs, did the first stab of realization slam into their souls—"This isn't what I thought it was going to be"? Did they realize they'd glutted themselves on sin and all mankind with them?

We don't know. We only know that remorse and repentance didn't quickly follow. When God asked, "What is this you have done?" the response wasn't, "I've sinned," or "I got so caught up in myself that I forgot about You. Forgive me."

Instead, Adam and Eve finger-pointed and blame-shifted. And as they were banished from the garden, the beauty of creation began to wither as they walked into sin's curse and left paradise behind. Fig leaves or no fig leaves, Eve and Adam left the garden stripped of everything.

ETERNAL ECHOES

One conversation in the garden of Eden changed humanity forever. It changed history forever. It set the world at war and launched a battle for truth that would rage for all generations to come. But Satan hadn't won. God had a plan in place through His Son, Jesus Christ, to reestablish our position with God, to secure our spiritual protection and power through the Holy Spirit, to promote our welfare and take back the blessings Satan plunders from our lives.

From the moment of the fall, communication with God and with ourselves radically changed. Our discernment became tainted and twisted by sin, and our self-talk became distorted. The serpent laid down a soundtrack in our hearts, and the voice of the Lord became obscured by variations on a theme that took root in Eve's soul: Gag God. Oppose God. Outwit God. Equal God. Become your own god.

The good news is that Satan didn't win. We have a Savior who fought the battle on our behalf and won. Through the power of His Holy Spirit, we can know the Sovereign God of truth intimately. God offers us the opportunity for a personal relationship with Jesus Christ and the promise that His righteousness covers what branches and leaves could not—the transfer of our sin for Jesus' perfect righteousness. He can transform our hearts and minds, but we must gear up, step up, and fight.

We must learn to listen to what we say to ourselves.

We must learn to evaluate our twisted and selfish motives and goals.

We must become committed to living out the double love command, a lifestyle that places love for God first and love of others second out of our overflow of God's love.

We must learn to walk moment by moment in faith and repentance and to say no to temptations to choose selfishly.

As we do, we will discern the voice of the Spirit of God calling to our spirit, speaking words of love as He transforms us into the image of His beloved Son from the inside out, one day at a time.

Jesus' voice calls to us with the promises of hope and the assurance of a transformed life and restored intimacy and fellowship with God. We can experience renewed minds. We can walk in a transformed vision of who God created us to be. And we can become conduits of authentic blessing in the lives of others.

> *Show me your ways, O Lord, teach me your paths; guide me in your truth and teach me, for you are God my Savior, and my hope is in you all day long.*
>
> —Psalm 25:4–5

Soul Search
Breaking the Silence

- Which of Satan's "whispers" resonates most through your life?
  - Gagging God
  - Opposing God
  - Outwitting God
  - Equaling God
- How do you struggle in the above areas? What means of defense do you use to handle your battles?
- What circumstances in your life do you believe have contributed to lies gaining power over your thinking? You may want to turn to appendix 3 for a further resource.

Facing the Seduction
Listening to the Spirit and the Word

Turn to appendix 5. For each of the following questions, consider designating several days to prayer and meditation, asking the Holy Spirit to spotlight specific areas of conflict in your battle with soul whispers.

Consider using the following Scriptures as you pray:

1 John 1:9	Psalm 86:1–13
Proverbs 28:13	Psalm 119:9–16

1. When I think about God, my thoughts are generally great thoughts about His sovereignty, goodness, holiness, mercy, and great love for me. Or, when I think about God, I think of unfairness, judgment, and His tolerance or anger.
2. It's okay to sometimes do and say things that contradict what's in the Bible.
3. I struggle with wanting to come up with my own plans apart from God or in opposition to God in the following areas:
   - finances
   - marriage, widowhood, or singleness
   - children
   - relationships with relatives and friends
   - job
   - future
   - past—forgiveness, reconciliation, restitution
   - stewardship of what God's given me—time, talent, money, resources, relationships
   - level of respect in dealing with people and regarding them as image-bearers

- control of my body—weight, addictions, stewardship of physical and emotional health
- control of my emotions
- control of my tongue
- a lifestyle of faith and repentance

4. I know biblical truth but choose to do something else often/seldom/frequently.
5. The motives and goals behind desires may be good or bad. Think of examples of when you've displayed good and bad motives and goals in fulfilling desires.
6. What selfish attitudes and choices has the Holy Spirit revealed to you? What whispers echo through your self-talk that urge you to sin in these areas?

RESPONDING FROM THE HEART
Prayer

Dear Father, I admit that it's difficult for me to see my weaknesses and self-deceptions. It's a lot easier for me to look at someone else and see their sin problems. But I'm asking You today to show me where I've offended people, where I've harbored bitterness and anger, where I've manipulated and controlled people and circumstances. I submit each area of my life to You as You reveal it to me, asking Your Holy Spirit to move in me to redeem my thinking.

Show me areas where I need to face true guilt and experience repentance, and help me deal with the voices of false guilt that keep me from moving forward in my life. Your Word tells us that when we repent and turn from our sin, You no longer see it. Help me forgive myself and to move into the life You envision for me.

Thank You for a love that reaches beyond condemnation to transformation. Amen.

CHAPTER 5

The POWER *of Living in the IF:*

Expectancy, Soul Change, and Philippians 2

Expectancy is the atmosphere for miracles.

—Edwin Louis Cole

In the movie *What Women Want,* actor Mel Gibson plays a womanizing advertising executive who suddenly finds himself able to read the minds of females. At first, he uses his ability to indulge his selfish interests but later grows into a kinder, gentler version of himself.

Imagine how the world would be different if we'd all been born with the ability to read the thoughts of everyone around us.

I, for instance, wouldn't have children because I wouldn't have a husband. On our first date (if I'd ever even gotten a date), Dan would have run screaming for his life. One peek at my self-talk would have revealed the dark side of me I work so hard to keep hidden—

The superficial me.

The proud me.

The selfish me.

The manipulative me . . . yet someone in love with her Father, someone learning to nestle more deeply into His arms each day.

And if I'd been able to read Dan's self-talk, I'd probably have run for the hills, too. The truth is, at the core of us, our struggles look pretty much the same because of our shared sin nature. Our skulls do a pretty good job of hiding our internal struggles with hypocrisy, lying, backbiting, slandering, gossiping, cheating, lust, laziness, gluttony, envy . . . need I go on?

It's easy to find examples if we're willing to look. A friend loses fifteen pounds, and the voices begin to whisper as we suddenly wrestle with jealousy or guilt. Something inside us yearns to grab a little of their joy and take it for ourselves.

Or we hear that someone who's hurt us has lost their job, and we feel a *zing* of pride and self-satisfaction. A voice whispers that maybe, just maybe, God's giving them what they deserved.

Or perhaps our boss doesn't give us the credit we believe we deserve, so we tell a few people what a tyrant he is and convince ourselves we're just standing up for our rights.

We all make excuses for our choices—logic and rationalization woven together with Satan's lies and our dreams for the life we're trying to create. Our self-talk is the script we write that ties our worldview together—the good, bad, and ugly, drafted and redrafted through our inner dialogues. Through this internal script, we assign meaning to our world, our circumstances, and ourselves.

Satan's agenda is to blind us to our self-centered goals and self-promoting spirits. Those attitudes begin in our thoughts and work their way into our conversations and actions. But the fact is, good resides in us, too. Christ has called us to a life of righteousness, a destiny "in which you shine like stars in the universe as you hold out the word of life—in order that I may boast on the day of Christ that I did not run or labor for nothing" (Philippians 2:15–16).

So how can people who struggle so deeply with ambition and twisted motives be commended as righteous and shining "like stars"? If the silent seduction of self-talk is inescapable, how are we supposed to deal with it?

LEANING INTO THE *IF*

British jockey Anthony Knott is a man who leaned into the power of possibilities for close to three decades. After twenty-eight years competing without a win, the forty-four-year-old father of three finally pulled his first victory out of the bag in November of 2008.

Years of near-victories and injuries nearly stripped him of his dream, but with each disappointment, the power of the *if* pulled him back into the race once again.

"Twenty-eight years is a long time to wait for a victory. I just wanted to win one race," Knott shared. He'd competed in dozens of events. Several of his horses had sustained injuries, and he'd never placed higher than fifth in any event and typically finished last.

Until he bought a six-year-old male named Wise Men Say.

"I think we were just underdogs sticking together."

In spite of his losses, Knott had maintained a grueling training schedule that included running, swimming, and circuit training, in addition to getting up at 3:30 every morning to milk his dairy herd.[3]

Why did he do it?

Anthony Knott possessed an attitude of expectancy.

He chose to live the life of a jockey and didn't allow his circumstances or people's attitudes toward his failures to define him. His self-talk could have easily convinced him to give up.

> *Why even bother? After so many years of losing, how can I expect to win?*
>
> *I'm just a dairy farmer wasting his time and money running after a stupid dream.*
>
> *Everyone probably thinks I'm crazy anyway, and why wouldn't they? I'm sneaking up on fifty, and I can't keep this up forever. Why not just throw in the towel?*

But instead of listening to his inner blather, Anthony took a stand against negative self-talk. He refused to let his mind run down dead-end paths and into the thickets of worry, self-doubt, fear, and a victim mentality.

The result? He stood in his irons to celebrate and wave to the crowd as they heralded his victory with a massive roar.

When we cross the threshold of decision, we have the power to change our mind-set. Details and circumstances that appear to be impediments fade into the background when a sense of expectancy hovers over us.

Our self-talk changes.

We see possibilities.

We see hope.

And if we are believers, we can learn to see past the temporal to the eternal.

We can learn to live in a state of anticipation—to live in the *if* of Philippians chapter 2—a life of expectancy in Jesus Christ.

SECRETS OF LIVING IN THE *IF*: THE FACTS

Expectancy. Anticipation.

What do you picture at the mention of those words?

Perhaps the anticipation of a woman with her hand resting on her womb, swollen with a growing child.

Or the look of a groom as his eyes lock on his bride as she glides toward his waiting arms.

What about a new father's intake of breath as he leans down and sweeps his newborn child into his arms?

Now envision that father as God and the child as you—a child with the power to stir His heart, to touch His heart like a newborn baby being cradled by her daddy.

You possess a gift that defies explanation—the ability to bring God joy. Although God is infinite and does not need us, He's chosen to link His emotions to ours. His love for us is so extravagant that Scripture tells us He grieves when we grieve (John 11:33–36), and our passions move His (Jonah 3:9–10). Proverbs 11:20 tells us the Lord "delights" in those whose ways are blameless. The Hebrew word here is *ratsown* and means to be pleased, to favor, and to experience pleasure.[4] Psalm 69:30–31 states that our praise pleases the Lord more than offerings, using the word *ya tab,* which means to make happy. Deuteronomy 10:14–15 further spells out the link between God's sovereignty and His incomprehensible affection for those He loves: "To the Lord your God belong the heavens, even the highest heavens, the earth and everything in it. Yet the Lord set his affection on your forefathers and loved them, and he chose you, their descendants, above all the nations, as it is today."

Imagine how life would change if we leaned into the *if* of God's intimate love for us with lives of expectancy. Would our self-talk change? Our choices? Would expectancy sweep away our fears as we envisioned the lives we were meant to live—charged with spiritual possibilities beyond our wildest dreams?

Philippians chapter 2 tells us how to step into this life of expectancy—life lived in the *if*—and not only change the way we view our world from the inside out, but to delight the heart of God.

LIFE IN THE *IF*

So how do we live lives of expectancy, take our thoughts captive, and learn to love God and others with all our hearts, souls, and minds, when voices deep inside us urge us to protect ourselves, position ourselves for the best possible advantage, promote ourselves, and grab for power?

The answer is found in four simple facts and the conditional word *if*—a "put-up-or-shut-up" kind of word that assumes we all make choices based on what we truly believe.

So what choices are we asked to make? If we're believers, the command to love God and love others shouldn't be so hard, right? But the reality of what we say we believe and how we live life often don't match. The questions posed in Philippians 2:1 are simple: Who do you *really* believe Christ is? Does what you say you believe reach all the way through your soul and shape the way you think and act?

Philippians 2 shows us the power of soul-saturated believing that produces a mind-set of servanthood. Growing into that mind-set begins by wrapping our minds in four simple facts, then absorbing them as the motivating forces in our lives.

> FACT NUMBER ONE: *"If you have any encouragement from being united with Christ . . ."* (v.1).

Imagine for a moment the sheer hopelessness of jumping without a parachute from an airplane at an altitude of 30,000 feet and plummeting toward a sure death to the ground below. Desperation swallows you as you feel the door of the plane open and the force of the air pummel your body as you prepare to step into the abyss of space and hurtle to your death.

Now imagine that at the final second you're offered the opportunity to strap yourself to an expert parachutist and be swept safely to the ground below. Your salvation rests in uniting your body to his and releasing control to his expert guidance.

With the offer of salvation, would mind-numbing gratitude surge through you? What about a changed attitude, or a new perspective on the life that's been restored to you?

Philippians 1:1 promises that God's children are united to Christ in an irrevocable, inseparable spiritual union that not only saves us from certain death, but ensures indescribable spiritual riches in this life and in heaven. Considering what we're promised in this verse, the word "encouragement" seems quite the understatement. The promise that we're stuck with God's own duct tape to Jesus Himself should revolutionize the way we act, live, and talk—to ourselves and others—if we live life in the reality of the *if*—with gushing, oozing, splattering gratitude that we're united with Jesus Christ and saved from certain death.

FACT NUMBER TWO: "*. . . if any comfort from his love . . .*" (v. 1).

The apostle Paul, the author of the book of Philippians, smacks us in the face with that little word *if* again.

Are we comforted by Christ's love? He's not with us physically, so what does that comfort look like on a day-to-day basis? Can we see it, feel it, touch it?

The word used for "comfort" here is the Greek word *paramuthemomai* and means to calm and console or to provide encouragement.[5] So the question the apostle Paul is asking us is, on a day-to-day basis, does the love of Jesus calm us, encourage us, console us?

"Of course," we answer. That's the right answer, isn't it?

The truth is our comfort—
nothing can touch us that doesn't
first pass through His loving hands.

But when gossip cuts us to the quick, are we tempted to retaliate with a rolling of the eyes, a sarcastic comment . . . or are we content to let Christ's love for us be our comfort? Instead, do we allow the indulgence of rationalizing self-talk to layer bitterness over our wounds, to infest our thoughts with criticism as we compare ourselves to those who've hurt us as we focus on their faults?

If the love of Jesus comforts us, we can turn away from negative self-talk, knowing we're wrapped in His perfect love. The truth is our comfort—nothing can touch us that doesn't first pass through His loving hands. The truth is our confidence that we're His chosen children, beloved, forgiven, free to forgive—in spite of what circumstances look like or what others may say or do.

But experiencing God's comfort is more than passively sitting and waiting for truth and positive emotions to flow through us. God's comfort energizes us. It draws us into a walk of faith that grows stronger with each step we take toward the cross. Second Corinthians 5:14–17 tells us that "Christ's love compels us, because we are convinced that one died for all, and therefore all died. And he died for all, that those who live should no longer live for themselves but for him who died for them and was raised again. . . . Therefore, if anyone is in Christ, he is a new creation; the old has gone, the new has come!"

Jesus' love is a motivating factor in my life that pulls me out of myself and into a life of servanthood—in my motives, goals, conversations, thinking, attitudes, choices. As I look at the sheer beauty of creation and the ultimate beauty of the cross, my thoughts race with the thrill of expectancy and gratitude as I lean into the *if*, knowing I'm called to a life of eternal purpose—with my eyes set on God's goals.

When God's goals are mine, my reactions aren't determined by how others treat me. Other people don't control my self-talk or my deeds. Because Jesus' love comforts and encourages me, I'm filled and led by the Spirit, and motivated to live an impossible life—a life that's beyond myself.

FACT NUMBER THREE: "*. . . if any fellowship with the Spirit . . .*" (v. 1).

Paul's third attitude-altering *if* acknowledges our life-changing fellowship with the Holy Spirit. For God's children, the indwelling and fellowship of the Holy Spirit are facts. The Greek word *koinonia* means to share or to have communication with—not an Internet chat type of connection, but the kind of face-to-face, heart-to-heart conversation that keeps friends talking into the wee hours of the night. But the Holy Spirit does more than communicate with us. He shares His power with us and creates fellowship among us as a body of believers.

The implications are staggering for our self-talk. The Holy

Spirit is speaking to us. He moves within us, communicates with us, enables us to do the will of God the Father. The Spirit of God shares His power with us, and we can tap into it through a personal relationship with Jesus. If we know Him as personal Savior, we have access to God the Father and can approach Him in continual conversation as we live to love Him and love others with all our heart, soul, and mind and strive to "work out [our] salvation with fear and trembling," knowing that it is "God who works in [us] to will and to act according to his good purpose" (Philippians 2:12–13).

Fellowship with the Spirit means we have access to God every moment of our lives through intimate communication. As we grow in a constant flow of conversation with God, our self-talk changes. We become more aware of His presence, priorities, and plans for our life, and we begin to live in the power of the *if* of Philippians 2:1. Knowing we have fellowship with the Spirit of God means we have all we'll ever need to live the life God envisioned for us . . . *if* we tap into God's inexhaustible resources and cultivate an attitude of expectancy for what He desires to do through us.

FACT NUMBER FOUR: *". . . if any tenderness and compassion . . ."* (v. 1).

Our final encouragement to live in anticipation is God's promise to transform us into people of tenderness and compassion. He promises to change our proud and stubborn hearts and make us like His Son, Jesus Christ. One of the evidences of the work of God in our lives is tenderheartedness—the overflow of our love for God as we love others. When God's Spirit is working in us, He breaks our hearts and gives us a deep and life-changing response to pain and suffering. Like Jesus, we become kind, empathetic, and easily moved by the plight of the poor and suffering.

God's greatest gift to us is the gift of change—the promise that we can become people with hearts like Jesus, hearts that beat with His, with voices that speak His truth and move with His thoughts. Philippians 2:1 ends with this final mind-boggling promise: *If* we unite our life to Christ's and step out in faith and obedience, the Spirit of God will revolutionize our hearts from the inside out.

CHANGE FROM THE INSIDE OUT: BECOMING LIKE JESUS

Philippians 2:2 expresses one of the most profound statements of our identity in Christ in Scripture: "Then make my joy complete . . ." The apostle Paul speaks these words, but they also represent the heart of God for our lives, and the thought is astounding.

> *"By being like-minded, having the same love, being one in spirit and purpose. Do nothing out of selfish ambition or vain conceit, but in humility consider others better than yourselves. Each of you should look not only to your own interests, but also to the interests of others. Your attitude should be the same as that of Christ Jesus: Who, being in very nature God, did not consider equality with God something to be grasped, but made himself nothing, taking the very nature of a servant, being made in human likeness. And being found in appearance as a man, he humbled himself and became obedient to death—even death on a cross! Therefore God exalted him to the highest place and gave him the name that is above every name, that at the name of Jesus every knee should bow, in heaven and on earth and under the earth; and every tongue confess that Jesus Christ is Lord, to the glory of God the Father.*
>
> —PHILIPPIANS 2:2–11

Today God invites us to join Him in a dance of joy, to anticipate His steps and to trust Him. He gives us the opportunity to choose humility, to look to the interests of others, and to choose Jesus' attitude—the attitude of a servant—even in our most difficult circumstances.

God's invitation slips under our door in a thousand forms. It came for my friend Susan with a call from an emergency room nurse telling Susan her eighty-nine-year-old mother had fallen and broken her hip. Could Susan drive six hours through the night to be with the mother who'd abused her as a child, accused her of criminal activities to Susan's siblings and family members, and had cut her out of her life just three years earlier? And then the nurse's final statement.

"After your mother's rehab, she shouldn't go back to her apartment to live. She told us she'll be making arrangements to live with you."

In the first shocking moment of those words, a wave of anger flooded through Susan. But during the six-hour drive to the hospital, she chose to lean into the anticipation of the *if.*

She focused on God's great forgiveness, His faithfulness, and her treasures in Christ.

Today God invites us to join Him in a dance of joy, to anticipate His steps and to trust Him.

She claimed her mother's accident as a gift—a time for healing in her own heart, even if her mother never moved toward restoration.

She focused on God's great gift of love for her.

Over the next three months, Susan took responsibility for her mother's care and eventually moved her mom into her home before she passed away due to complications from her fall. And while those months were challenging, Susan found peace as she poured God's love out on a mother whose heart never softened.

How did Susan do it? Not through her own strength. She knew, first of all, that her power came through Jesus, who's accomplishing His will in the universe in spite of what she could see.

Second, Susan allowed Jesus' love to comfort her—a love that compelled her to love a mother who never knew how to love her back.

Third, Susan knew the power available to her every moment in order to minister through those three difficult months. She had direct access to God through the power of the Holy Spirit.

Last of all, Susan was willing to be changed. During those months, she grew more like Jesus in tenderness and compassion. She knew her moments with her mother were infused with eternal purpose and that God had chosen her before the foundation of the world to minister love to her mother. She was on a holy mission to reflect God's glory and lived each day with expectancy, knowing she was partnering with God.

Living in the *if* means strapping ourselves to the reality of Philippians chapter 2 and leaping from the plane at 30,000 feet. It means living our lives *as if* all that Jesus said and did were really true. It means taking captive our thoughts and wrapping them around the truth of the Word of God. It means taking on the hard work of working out our salvation with fear and trembling.

If we're willing to face who we are.

And *if* we're willing to take the plunge into a life of servanthood.

SOUL SEARCH
Breaking the Silence

- Do you struggle with voices of comparison and self-criticism? How does this affect your life? Where do you think these thoughts originate?
- Do you struggle with thoughts of pride and comparing yourself to others? How does this affect your life? Where do you think these thoughts originate?
- Is a judgmental and critical spirit evidenced in your self-talk or in your conversation with others? In what ways? How does this

influence your ability to love people? To love yourself?

- Do you struggle with a defensive or rationalizing attitude, rather than taking responsibility? How does this play out in your self-talk? How is it evidence of a lie? How does it block you from loving others?
- Evaluate each of the areas above for an extended period of time and take notes on your negative self-talk. Ask yourself, "What am I really telling myself? What seems to be my underlying motive? Is it self-protection, self-promotion, positioning, procuring power, plundering, or something else, such as fear or false guilt?" Then write down the true biblical perspective on that subject. Conform your thoughts around the Word as you meditate on God's true perspective.

FACING THE SEDUCTION
Listening to the Spirit and the Word

1. Consult appendix 6 and read through the exercise. You may want to use a notebook to record your answers.
2. Read Deb's letter below.
    - Why do you think she was deceived about her self-image?
    - What factors contributed to how she felt?
    - What did God use to change her thinking?
    - Imagine you were Deb. What specific changes in your self-talk would be necessary to begin seeing yourself as God sees you?

3. Consult appendix 10. Which of the promises and statements regarding our identity in Christ apply to Deb's letter? Do any of those statements resonate deeply with you? Why?

I WAS BORN INTO a family with a wide spectrum of emotional needs. My father was absent most of my life. I saw him twice a year, but his wife let me know I wasn't welcome even on those occasions. My mom faced intense struggles and turned to men and us kids with passive sexual manipulation and guilt to get what she thought she needed.

My being sexually abused started early, and I thought it was normal. I believed all men violated women and it was my fault. I had always felt unloved and unwanted and that I was a mistake. When I left home for my sophomore year of college, my stepdad reinforced what I'd heard from all other males in my life. "Don't come around anymore. Life is better without you in it. I never want to see you again."

I struggled with thoughts like, "You've had a hard life so God won't hold you accountable for the poor choices you're making." "You're worthless." "Nobody loves you." "You don't belong." "Life would be better without you in it."

Earlier in my life I'd accepted Jesus as my personal Savior. The truth hadn't penetrated my head or heart because I believed life on earth was a life I lived on my own. When I died I'd be allowed in heaven, but I didn't understand that God wanted a relationship with me now. Why would the God of the universe be interested in me if my own family couldn't understand me?

As my life progressed, God brought people alongside me who helped me journey through my pain, and I was able to forgive. God showed me the lies in my head were straight from the pit of hell, and I'm responsible for giving ground to the Enemy and allowing those thoughts to take root and grow. I learned to insert truth where lies were allowed to roam free. I sometimes stumble and fall, but God is faithful. He forgives and puts me back on track. Because of this, I've continued to grow and move forward.

The key for me has been Scripture.

Psalm 16:11: "You have made known to me the path of life; you will fill me with joy in your presence, with eternal pleasures at your right hand." It's been crucial for me to have intimate communion daily with the Lord in His Word, as I confess my sins and once again experience the grace He offers.

1 John 1:9–10: I'm responsible for my choices.

Psalm 86:13: I am loved.

John 3:16: I have inestimable worth.

John 15:5: God is doing a work in me.
Psalm 139: I belong and I'm not a mistake.
John 8:31–32: I'm set free.
Titus 3:5a: I'm the recipient of God's amazing mercy.

I walk in newness of life. If you knew me now, you'd be surprised that lies ruled my life. God wants to change us through the power of His love.

—Deb W.

Responding from the Heart
Prayer

Precious Father, thank You for a love so great that You pick me up when I'm wounded and broken and cradle me in Your arms. You have loved me with an everlasting love, stamping me with a price tag marked by Your Son's precious blood. You know me intimately. Sometimes my greatest struggle is the struggle with the weight of my guilt—believing that You would ever want to have me as Your follower.

Free me from the lie that says You're a God who loves me from a distance, who's aloof and doesn't care about my pain and problems. Today I want to pull myself up close to You, Lord, and pour out my heart. I give You the pain and the hurt. You've promised to show me the path of life and to fill me with joy in Your presence, and I ask for that today.

Help me to see my true identity in You, Lord. You created and crafted and designed me uniquely and have given me every spiritual blessing necessary to live the life of an overcomer through Your Son, Jesus. Today I claim my identity as Your beautiful and beloved child, fearfully and wonderfully made. I claim the gifts You have placed in me. Give me the wisdom and grace to use them for Your purposes. Bless me with fruitfulness to be a life-giver in the world as I pour out the life and hope and message of forgiveness so freely poured out in my life. Amen.

CHAPTER 6

RECLAIMING *Our Legacy:*

Philippians 4:4–9

Nobody ever did, or ever will, escape the consequences of his choices.

—ALFRED A. MONTAPERT

"So why'd you give her the bullet if you knew she might put the gun to my head and pull the trigger someday?"

I sat, pale-faced, across the table from a colleague as his question jolted my heart. I'd asked him to come to my office so I could tell him about a conversation I'd had with someone in our organization—someone neither of us trusted. My friend had made a professional decision, and I'd discussed it with a colleague.

Moments after I opened my mouth, I felt guilty. Unfortunately, it was an all-too-familiar feeling. For two days the Holy Spirit pummeled my heart. My brief conversation with a colleague had cast a shadow over my friend who was now forced to live with the consequences of my selfish choice.

I struggled to answer his challenge.

Words came to my lips—something partially true with a few lame rationalizations. But my colleague's question cut to the heart of my motives.

Why *would* I provide ammunition I knew might annihilate the reputation of a trusted friend? Why hadn't I spoken to my friend directly?

Before I'd ever spoken to my supervisor, a vague sense of guilt had gnawed at me, but I'd covered up my uneasiness with a veneer of excuses. My self-talk assured me I was motivated by the good of the organization.

But self-talk can be deceiving, and veneer, when pulled away, reveals stark realities no one wants to see. My friend's question ripped away the veneer with one painful jerk.

The truth was, I'd sensed our colleague would most likely probe and come to negative conclusions. And I knew she was known to pack heat and have a trigger finger. Yet I'd willingly handed over a bullet.

I stammered out a heartbroken apology, knowing I couldn't reverse the consequence of what I'd done.

But the reality of what I'd done hung over my heart for months afterward.

Why had I made such a selfish choice? How could I have convinced myself to do such a stupid, self-centered thing?

I was terrified to admit the answer, even in the privacy of my own thoughts. But I finally faced the truth.

Beneath the excuses, I'd been motivated by a desire to protect myself and position myself positively in front of my supervisor. Deep inside, I'd been motivated by pure, unadulterated selfishness.

I'M NOT OKAY, YOU'RE NOT OKAY

Pure, unadulterated selfishness—it's the ugly taproot that feeds our motivation to sin. It's what makes me just like you and you just like me.

Five years ago I wouldn't have thought more than a moment or two about my conversation with my supervisor after I'd had it. My yammering rationalizations and mental gymnastics were drowning out the voice of the Holy Spirit.

One day I found my face planted in the mud and grime of my

life and suddenly realized I'd spent most of my life playing word games about how much I loved God and people.

It was a painful, glorious day—the day I realized God loved me enough to put a plan in place to change me. And it was the day I asked God to begin stripping away the veneer of my soul.

Layers of pride and indifference were peeled back as I searched Scripture and prayed. But I also journaled and studied my self-talk. I asked for discernment and wisdom to see myself in a new way—my emotions, will, and how old wounds had shaped my thinking. I asked God to help me recognize strongholds and to break them.

As I prayed, God began to reveal threads of my self-talk that seemed outrageously godless. I could hear my own thoughts and hit a *pause* button on my manipulation, anger, ingratitude, or judgmental spirit. Some days I couldn't make it to the refrigerator without a Holy Spirit gong going off in my head like a four-alarm fire. I began to pray over conversations before I spoke and replayed scenarios after my interactions, evaluating not just the things I said, but the things I wanted to say. As I evaluated my speech and my self-talk, I asked God to give me a biblical perspective on the motives behind my words and actions.

One prayer at a time, God began to show me what I'd been begging to see. Slowly my self-talk journal filled. I confessed bitterness, anger, envy, and discontent. I saw how I'd obscured my motives with busyness, pride, and rationalization.

But for the first time in my life, instead of being crushed by guilt for my sin, I felt exhilaration. With each new revelation and confession, I felt a surge of hope.

God was talking to me. He was answering my prayers. He was changing me.

Self-talk that had once seemed random had become a stream of prayer. My communication with God had gone from a few points of time in my day to a steady stream of conversation.

Praise.

Requests.

Thanks.

Chitchat about the events of my day.

Confession and repentance.

Then one day, like light in a swamp, a realization dawned.

Self-talk isn't private. God shares it all with us—the good, the bad, and the ugly.

Although at first glance it wasn't a profound thought, I saw for the first time that self-talk was a means of intimate communication with God. As His children, we have the privilege of both listening to the Spirit and initiating communication with the Spirit. Whether we've just been awarded Woman of the Year or yelled at the car that just cut us off in traffic, God is present in our thoughts. A flash of pride or guilt is an opportunity for immediate confession and restoration. Moments of joy are chances to heap gratitude on a good and loving God.

We were meant to live in a state of constant communion and growth as our spirit is quickened by God's. Tapping into the power of our self-talk is a direct line between our heart and the Father's.

GOD'S ALL-SEEING MIRROR

One of my favorite TV shows puts everyday people inside a three-hundred-and-sixty-degree mirror for a fashion reality check. Confidence usually melts from participants' faces as they're forced to take a long look at their true reflection in multi-imaged detail. More often than not, the image inside their heads doesn't match the reality they project on the outside.

Often, the image inside our heads doesn't line up with the image we're projecting to the world around us. The truth of the matter is that at the core of our being, we know we're broken people living in a broken world. We wish we were better persons, and we live with the nagging sense that we fall short. We recognize we're imperfect, and disappointment and shame are part of our daily struggle. Our self-talk is often a reflection of the conflicting emotions that tear at our spirits—our aspirations for the good and the true, knotted with tangled threads of guilt and disappointment.

The path to redeeming our self-talk is to figure out when we're lying to ourselves and when we're trying to outsmart God.

Before Eden ever existed, God set a plan in place that would release the world from the bondage of guilt. Jesus' death on the cross redeemed not only our spirits, but our bodies and minds from the curse of sin. But His gift of salvation doesn't free us from responsibility for renewing our minds and choosing right actions (see Romans 12:2). The path to redeeming our self-talk is to figure out when we're lying to ourselves and when we're trying to outsmart God. Our job is to become students of our sinful, sassy selves, then to evaluate our motives and goals under the authority of the Word of God and the Spirit of God.

I spoke with a friend this week—a leader in his church and a man who's studied the Bible for most of his fifty years. He was sharing details of a messy union-employee situation at his job and commented how he'd used a loophole in a union rule to create a job crisis for his boss. His tone, facial expression, and words told me how much he'd enjoyed "sticking it" to his superior. I was curious about how he'd arrived at his conclusion that his behavior was acceptable to God, and so I decided to ask.

"Tell me, when you were deciding to get your boss in trouble with his boss, did you think about your motives at all? How do you think your actions fit into the whole 'love your neighbor as yourself thing?' " I asked.

"Motives? Love? You're kidding, right? It felt good to give this guy a little grief. He's a jerk."

"People can sure act that way. But does the Bible ever comment about how believers are supposed to act toward the 'jerks' of the world?"

He laughed. "Get real. We're talking about the union here. Besides, I used the rules somebody handed me. This guy finally got back some of the garbage he'd been handing out for the past twenty years."

We chatted for a few more minutes and moved on in our conversation. Apparently Scripture that related to how believers are to respond when persecuted, our responsibility to love our enemies, or what it means to have a humble spirit didn't seem to apply to everyday life for my friend. His motive was clear: payback. Scriptural principles were irrelevant—something Bible characters were responsible to live out, or maybe famous Christian missionaries or his pastor. Or maybe he believed that biblical principles only applied to certain situations in life.

My friend's thinking was spiritually schizophrenic, just like mine had been for so many years and still can be. Just like yours. We all do battle with dueling truths. It's the nature of sin and the nature of self-talk.

Yes, I know the Bible says that. No, I don't think it applies to me today.

Until we peel back the layers of our self-talk, our spiritual growth will be stunted. We can only grow in proportion to our awareness of our hidden motives as we become self-conscious sinners committed to a lifestyle of repentance and faith. And as the Spirit of God moves in us and we fall more deeply in love with Jesus, He empowers us to more fully love others.

THE WEEDS IN THE GARDEN

Self-talk can take the form of harmless babble. It can also serve as an instrument of blessing, grace, and creativity. But self-talk can also encase core motives attached to demanding attitudes or feelings of guilt we inherited when Adam and Eve left the garden. Nothing they could do from the moment of their sin would ever be right again; everything was tainted. Even the most glorious moments of their lives after the fall were overshadowed by fear, condemnation, remorse, the "if onlys" of life.

From the moment sin entered the world, our self-talk became a tangle of dreams, aspirations, creativity, disappointments, regrets, truth, lies, and noble and twisted motives. We were created to live in intimate fellowship with God, to bring Him joy, and to bless His creation. But our misplaced motives got in the way, and they've blocked intimate fellowship with God ever since.

Discernment is our most powerful weapon in our war to break free from the silent seduction of self-talk, and God has told us we can ask for it. The list below can help us recognize some of the motivating sins that can trap us.

Anger: at God, at people, at ourselves; for circumstances, pain, conflict, feelings we've gotten a raw deal

Bitterness: deep resentment stemming from anger

Blame: a sense of "holding responsible"
- blaming ourselves
- blaming others
- blaming God
- refusing to accept blame

Deceit: lying to God
- lying to ourselves about who God is, who I am, who others are
- lying to others

Envy: antagonism toward someone because of something good they have that you don't

Idolatry: placing anything or anyone in God's place

Jealousy: fear, suspicion, or envy because one's possessions appear to be threatened

Misplacing responsibility: evading
- taking from others or God

Payback or revenge: for circumstances, pain, conflict, feeling we've gotten a raw deal

Perversion of the truth: who I am, who God is, who others are, what my responsibilities are to God, His children, and the world

Plundering from others: their position, authority, possessions, relationships

Positioning and pride: making myself look good; elevating myself above the interests of others and of God

Rebellion: opposition to God

Self-gratification: sexual, material, or financial, pride, hedonism

THE PROMISE OF HOPE

As God's children, we still struggle and contend—with each other and within ourselves. The apostle Paul refers to the disagreements of Euodia and Syntyche, his friends in the faith, in Philippians 4. Apparently these women were causing conflict in the church because of disagreements with each other. And conflicts in churches today reflect their struggles. Statistics tell us that between 1,400 to 1,600 spiritual leaders are leaving the ministry each month, many because of conflict and disagreement.[6] This is staggering and paints a fairly hopeless picture. But Paul also presents hope for both our internal struggles and our struggles with others.

In verse 4 of chapter 4, Paul reminds his readers to stay focused. The Philippians, like us, struggled with family conflict, and financial challenges. They faced spiritual doubts, church debates, and wrestled with the complexities of broken relationships, jealousies, and depressions. They were like us in every way, but without the hassle of dropped cell phone calls and failed Internet connections. Paul's life-changing advice to them is the same advice that has the power to transform our self-talk.

Get Your Eyes on God

Philippians 4:4

Whether we realize it or not, a lot of us carry a giant crayon in our head. We use it to divide our lives into "God's space" and "my space." My friend did this when he convinced himself his decision to give his boss grief didn't have anything to do with his relationship with God. On one side of the crayon line were the principles of the Bible. On the other side were his reasons for not living them out.

But before you pass judgment on my friend, think back to a time when you've done the same thing. You might not have to look far—a time when someone smacked you down and you smacked back. A time when you walked away from a conversation knowing you'd slandered someone's reputation, and yet you gloated. A time when you savored the thought of someone's fall from grace because you were convinced you were better than they were.

Twice Paul tells the Philippians to rejoice in the Lord, and to do it *in spite of* their circumstances. Paul's confidence in God's infinite knowledge, unlimited power, and limitless love for him were at the heart of his ability to rejoice and to do good in spite of difficulties, trials, persecution, rejection, and even abandonment.

Imagine for a moment the self-talk Paul is asking us to actively focus our minds on. He's not asking us to stir up positive feelings. He's pointing us toward the reality of our faith and the core motive for all we think, all we do, all we say—we worship a God who can be trusted.

Even when life stinks.

Even when people fail us.

Even when we fail.

We can *choose* to rejoice, based on the object of our faith—an infinitely reliable, worthy, loving, sovereign God who's in charge of every detail of the universe, every cell of our bodies. The God who sacrificed His very Son for us is incapable of messing up our lives, even when our lives are a mess.

The word *rejoice* itself carries a weight of expectancy, infusing confidence in every thought stirring our hearts. Our destiny rests in the hands of an all-knowing, all-seeing, all-powerful God who loves us with a love that can't be comprehended by human thought.

What kind of self-talk does love like that inspire? What motives are evoked in response to a love so gargantuan it defies description?

But you're talking in spiritualities, you say. *My boss is treating me like dirt. How are we supposed to put skin on this?*

We rejoice by claiming truth in the middle of our crummy job circumstances—no matter the mess we see around us, God is at work in every detail, working out eternal purposes, far beyond what we could ever envision. We can walk in the truth that God has given us every resource to live a life of forgiveness, grace, and integrity, in spite of the personal cost. We can choose to rejoice, knowing we were placed in our job for eternal purposes—to be the light of the world (Matthew 5:14), that we were divinely placed and strategically chosen for this very moment. We can rejoice with a mind-set of anticipation and expectancy in all we do, knowing we're being used by God for eternal purposes.

We rejoice—not because of what's happening to us, but because we know we're eternally loved and secure in the middle of the mess. We rejoice because we're empowered to love others with an impossible love and live an impossible life in the middle of impossible challenges.

Wrapping our thoughts around the truth of who God truly is will revolutionize not only our self-talk, but our motives and goals in all we do as we walk out Jesus' love in our relationships with the people around us.

Live a Gentle Life in a Grasping World

Philippians 4:5

Spill a cup of hot coffee on your lap, and you've got the makings of a lawsuit. Stumble in a grocery store, and you could be cashing in on that cruise to the Bahamas you've been dreaming of. Branch from a neighbor's tree fall on your used minivan? One call to the right lawyer, and your next car might be a Lexus.

As a society, we live and die clinging to our rights, and our obsession with litigation demonstrates the ease with which we can sweep aside spiritual values with temporal ones.

A month ago my mother fell in the elder care facility where for nearly a year she and my father had been lovingly cared for. She struck her head, and a week later she died. As I described the circumstances of Mom's death to casual acquaintances, I was surprised by how many who asked if our family had considered suing. As a family, nothing could have been further from our minds. None of us could envision Mom's home going as being an instrument of contention.

But I'll have to admit that in the middle of my grief, it would have been easy to have allowed my thoughts to get swept along by accusation and anger, to have allowed the "what ifs" to have taken over. Instead, I made the same choice every member of my family made—to extend the same love to those who'd cared for my mom that I'd have desired for myself or loved ones.

We're instructed to show gentleness at all times, to all people, even when we think we have good reason to take matters into our own hands, send out an angry e-mail, even retort with a sarcastic comment. The Greek word for gentleness, *epieikes*, means to demonstrate patience and meekness in even the most difficult of circumstances. We don't insist on the letter of the law, even when it's within our power. We pursue a greater good—the love of Jesus.

Conforming means we wrap our thoughts around Jesus' immense love for us in order to demonstrate that love to others through the same grace and forgiveness we've been extended. Our actions begin in our thoughts and the decision to live gentle lives in a grasping world.

Not out of reluctance, but because Jesus is real. He's near, His Spirit resides in us, and He's promised to set right the wrongs of our upside-down world through His final redemption of all things (Ephesians 1:13b–14).

Make Prayer and Thanksgiving Your Moment-by-Moment Practice

Philippians 4:6

Have you ever felt so sidelined by anxiety that worry preoccupied your every thought?

The comic character in *What about Bob?* shows us an example of someone experiencing anxiety at a level that extends to the stratosphere. Bob's anxieties make it difficult for him to leave his apartment, to use elevators, or to be around people with everyday sniffles. Bob represents the anxiety-ridden person we're all capable of becoming if we don't keep our self-talk about the world's threatening possibilities in check. After all, we're all one heartbeat away from death, one germ away from infection, one computer glitch from plummeting to our death in an airliner.

Or are we?

Philippians 4:6 tells us, "Do not be anxious *about anything.*" Interesting words from a man who was writing while imprisoned and facing a possible death sentence. Philippians 1:13 refers to the *praetorium*, the palace guards, who were literally chained to his body. Paul wasn't spouting spiritual platitudes. He was sitting in the dirt and the dark without a flush toilet, stripped of everything he owned, separated from everyone who loved him, chained to someone sworn to be his enemy who had taken a blood oath to report his every word and movement.

And Paul's words as the hours ticked away toward his trial?

Rejoice. Don't be anxious. Not about a single thing.

And what did Paul model instead of hand-wringing, sleepless nights, stomach ulcers, and frazzled nerves?

Prayer. Petition. Thanksgiving.

Paul suggests the most practical approach to anxiety we could possibly be given. First of all, we're to come to God in simple prayer. The word that's used in the Greek in this passage expresses the key to transformed self-talk—our freedom to approach God boldly at any time, about any thing. The idea is simple: turn our conversation with ourselves into conversation with God.

In the Old Testament, the children of Israel were barred from the Holy of Holies where God's presence dwelt by a system of sacrifices, priests, and purification rituals. But after Jesus Christ's death on the cross, the curtain that separated the Holy of Holies was split. Mankind has had free access to God through Jesus from that moment on. We can now burst into forbidden rooms, approaching God with the boldness of a child racing through the house and climbing into her father's lap.

God is as accessible to us as a whisper or a thought. We no longer have to prove ourselves through sacrifices, good works, or achievement. We can blast through the Holy of Holies and run straight into Abba's arms and pour out our prayers, knowing He tips His ear in anticipation, waiting to hear our heartaches, longings, fears, dreams, and regrets.

But Paul doesn't leave us with a general encouragement to prayer. He tells us to come to God with our petitions or requests. In fact, he makes the statement twice, reminding us to bring our requests "with thanksgiving." He reminds us we should always be thankful for the character of God, knowing that, in spite of what circumstances may look like on the surface, God works out purposes that extend beyond what we can see and that always work out for our good.

If we evaluate our self-talk, we'll likely discover that much of what we're saying falls into the category of anxiety—worry about our kids, grandkids, parents, spouse, unpaid bills, boss, family responsibilities, health, the economy, or how we're going to stave off the inevitabilities of old age. We may even have difficulty sleeping at night as our minds whirl and we make endless lists. I know I've been there.

Controlling our self-talk in the face of cancer, bankruptcy, divorce, or a call in the middle of the night to bail our child out of jail can be overwhelming. But Philippians 4:6 provides a weapon in the war—running to God in prayer with our petitions and requests, and layering our prayers with thanksgiving for God's character and sufficiency.

Self-talk that's centered on prayer isn't self-talk at all. It's conversation. God promises not only to talk back, but to change us in the process.

God Promises the Results—Peace that Transcends Understanding

Philippians 4:7–9

As we take steps in learning to live a life of moment-by-moment prayer, we gain confidence that God's at work bringing about good things in our lives. Our prayers remind us that God knows every detail of our lives, and He cares. Our prayers remind us He's always listening, He's interested, and He's active in our lives. They remind us He wants to hear from us, no matter how big or small our concerns or requests. Our prayers change our focus and teach us to rejoice in who God is and what He's already done for us. They cultivate a grateful heart, a mark of our spiritual maturity.

As we learn to talk to God on a moment-by-moment basis, we learn to rejoice in difficult life circumstances. We open the door for Him to renew our hearts. We begin to rest in God's perfect peace and savor the truth that He provides everything we need, in spite of what our circumstances may look like. Our minds are freed from chains of negative self-talk, and we focus on higher things:

> *Finally, brothers, whatever is true, whatever is noble, whatever is right, whatever is pure, whatever is lovely, whatever is admirable—if anything is excellent or praiseworthy—think about such things. Whatever you have learned or received or heard from me, or seen in me—put it into practice. And the God of peace will be with you.*
>
> —Philippians 4:8–9

God knows our situation, and He'll work out even our most discouraging circumstances for our good. In spite of what we see, we're responsible to put admirable and praiseworthy motives into practice. We accomplish this by speaking to ourselves truthfully and by bringing our pain, offenses, and losses to the loving God who bears our burdens.

SPEAKING IN UPPERCASE

A friend of mine recently received a less-than-positive response from an editor regarding a manuscript she'd submitted. Another writer friend offered encouraging counteradvice: retype the response of the editor, putting his positive comments in capital letters and leaving his negative observations in lowercase.

The apostle Paul takes a similar approach in his letters to fellow believers. He states the challenges of his imprisonments, suffering, chains, and potential death sentences in "lowercase" perspective but always emphasizes the sufficiency and provision of God. It's impossible to read Paul's epistles without seeing God's sovereign control in His children's lives, no matter what life looks like on the outside.

What would your self-talk sound like if you sat chained to a guard, separated from loved ones, facing a likely death sentence? Would you be able to confidently ask others to follow your example as Paul did? "Whatever you have learned or received or heard from me, or seen in me—put it into practice" (Philippians 4:9).

Where does your self-talk typically lead you? To complaining, anxiety, bitterness, rebellion, jealousy, paybacks, manipulation, anger, blame, defensiveness, to withholding your gifts from others and God? Or does it lead to love and forbearance for others, to prayer and thanksgiving, and to a focus on things that are true, noble, right, pure, lovely, admirable, excellent, and praiseworthy?

Paul knew the importance of exploring the motives of his heart and saturating his thoughts with truth. Until we peel back the layers of our self-talk, we'll remain blind to our spiritual schizophrenia. But as we conform our thinking to God's Word, we'll experience the gift of change—new hearts and new motives as we become instruments of peace with others as we experience peace with God.

SOUL SEARCH
Breaking the Silence

- How or when have you seen evidence of hidden motives at work in your life—motives rooted in anger, bitterness, revenge, desires to hurt someone, or one of the other motives listed in this chapter? Do any of these motives have similar roots or patterns? For instance, do you struggle in general with anger at God or with bitterness toward people? Have you ever evaluated possible or contributing sources?
- Spend a concentrated period of time (perhaps a week) in prayer over the motives listed in this chapter and ask God to reveal which ones might be central to your life. List other motives you believe have grown from this primary motive, if any.
- If you have been struggling with a particular individual, begin to record the kinds of self-talk you tell yourself regarding this person: attitudes, feelings, rights that have been violated, what you think you're entitled to, etc. List the kinds of things you tell yourself are true about this person, about yourself in relation to this person, and your responsibilities to this person.
- Ask God to reveal self-indulgent attitudes and negative self-talk and show you how to begin to speak what is true, noble, right, pure, lovely, admirable, excellent, and praiseworthy in its place. Then consult your notes. Highlight the things you believe are negative in red and the things that would be true and praiseworthy in blue. Then assess yourself. What has been the general character of your self-talk in this situation or toward this person—negative and critical or God-honoring and praiseworthy?

FACING THE SEDUCTION
Listening to the Spirit and the Word

1. Read the book of Daniel chapters 1 and 2 and try to imagine the positive self-talk Daniel focused on that allowed him to rejoice in his difficult of circumstances. What do you think he told himself about his identity and what his role was in God's plan? What do you think he told himself about who God was and what his relationship was to God? What kind of relationship did Daniel appear to have with God, and how do you think this may have related to his self-talk?
2. What kinds of negative self-talk could have easily changed Daniel's interactions with those around him? What kinds of negative self-talk would you have most easily fallen into in Daniel's circumstances? How does your confidence in the awareness of God influence your self-talk on a day-to-day basis?
3. What does Daniel's prayer tell you about his focus on the character of God (Daniel 2:20–23)?
4. Turn to appendix 8 if you haven't already considered this valuable exercise in journaling to help you turn up the volume of your self-talk and discover your hidden motivations.

RESPONDING FROM THE HEART
Prayer

Dear Gracious God, make me more aware that You're with me in my self-talk and that every moment of my life is an opportunity to turn to You in prayer. Help me to turn to You the next time I hear the voices of anger or bitterness or a demanding spirit and to turn those moments into opportunities for conversation with You. May I see them as promptings from Your Spirit to turn to You and plead for forgiveness and a commitment to love, in spite of the price.

Thank You for a lavish love that You gave in spite of the price. Thank You for heaping my sins on Your Son, then taking the blame that should have been mine and heaping that upon Him all over again. I stand in awe of Your love for me, Father. May my heart be astonished every day by Your overwhelming love for me and respond in an outburst of love for others.

May I know the things You've called me to know and do the things You've called me to do. May I carry out Your work with honor, peace, and joy, confident that You're growing me in beauty of spirit and in the wisdom and knowledge of Your Son, Jesus. Amen.

CHAPTER 7

TUNING OUT *the Clamor:*

Considering, Wanting, Forgetting, and Straining

Beware lest clamor be taken for counsel.

—Desiderius Erasmus

The screaming was so loud I could barely hear myself think. But it was all part of the game.

Twenty or so of us had gathered around my friend Melva's table to play Spoons—a game that combined Pit, mind-numbing shouting, and a maniacal form of spoon grabbing with complete disregard for the number of fingers you hoped to retain for the rest of your life.

We were an unlikely group to be gathered for a game. Our ages ranged from five to sixty-eight, with a cluster of children hovering around the age of ten. The grandparents among us were a hearty lot and not intimidated by adrenaline-charged adolescents wielding cutlery. With each round of play, the decibel level grew higher and the spoons were grabbed with greater gusto.

At one end of the table Alvie and Norman sat side by side. Norman was my father-in-law, the quietest and most prayerful man to walk earthly streets this side of heaven's gates. Alvie was a family friend and rivaled Norman with his calm and gentle spirit. The two sat head-to-head amid the din, quietly exchanging cards with each other in voices so soft I assumed they must be lipreading. As the chaos of the game whirled around them, Norman and Alvie smiled and traded the same few cards back and forth. They never won a single hand all evening, but they were playing for bigger reasons. The game of Spoons wasn't about winning or losing.

They were there for the sake of family, even if it meant enduring ear-popping chaos.

For Norman and Alvie, the game of Spoons was about love.

CHOOSING CONTENTMENT IN THE CLAMOR

For most of us, life is a lot like a game of Spoons, with family and friends crowded around a table, shouting, elbowing, and grabbing at shiny objects life flashes in front of us. In spite of good intentions, family members get hurt, friends play by rules of their own making, and the game of life turns out to be an exercise in disappointment as everyone makes their best grab, and some of us come up short.

It doesn't take long to find ourselves whispering that we've been cheated, that life was supposed to have worked out better than this.

We deceive ourselves into thinking we could win in life if only God would deal us a better hand.

My husband's such a jerk. Walking out would solve my problems.

God's holding back the happiness I deserve, so it's up to me to get it on my own.

Nobody's experienced the abuse I've been through, and forgiving means condoning what was done to me.

Loving my neighbor is a nice thought, but I've got a family and a future to consider.

The idea of tithing is so "Old Testament," and God can't expect me to give when He doesn't provide enough money for me to pay my bills.

Most of us are masters at convincing ourselves that we come to the game of life with pure motives. But even our most seemingly innocent and virtuous acts can sometimes be motivated by selfishness.

LOOKING FOR THE STRONG SUIT

The game of Spoons, like most card games, requires players to swap cards to collect similar cards, or suits. Players build on their strongest suit to win.

While hundreds of factors contribute to our self-talk, several influential "suits" influence the way we approach life.

Voices of Family

Some families are rigid and rule-bound. One or both parents may have had an overbearing personality and shown little or no physical affection. Preferential treatment may have been shown for one child over another. Elements like these would certainly impact our security, significance, sense of feeling loved, perhaps even gender attitudes or our view of God.

The voices of family can speak love, comfort, affirmation, accusation, condemnation, shame to our souls. But the question we must ask is, "How have the voices of family shaped our self-talk?" How have they influenced our ability to love others, to love ourselves, and to love God? Have those voices fed God's truth, or have they fed lies? What impact have they had on our ability to be loving, compassionate, and Christlike individuals who relate authentically with others and who live out the double love command?

Did you grow up in a family with unclear boundaries or where parents were in conflict with one another? Did one parent undercut the authority of another? How did this influence your view of authority, ability to respect and relate to others, or ability to trust? How did your family relationships affect your view of marriage? God? trust?

The pull of broken family relationships were at work in the lives of biblical characters. Yet many of these men and women chose to love God and others in spite of the price. Jonathan, son of King Saul, pulled himself away from his father's influence and ignored his counsel to rebel against David so he himself could inherit the throne (1 Samuel 19:1). Naomi counseled her daughter-in-law Ruth to turn back to the nation of her birth and her family, but Ruth refused and, instead, devoted herself to following Naomi (Ruth 1). As a result, she reaped the rich blessings of Boaz's love and her place in the lineage of Jesus.

Voices of Culture and Tradition

Culture and tradition include factors as diverse as socioeconomics, ethnicity, education, and geography. Even the churches we've attended shape our self-talk.

My friend Carol and her husband recently joined a new church and are the only white couple in an African-American congregation. After a lifetime in white churches where promptness ruled, my friends are learning to readjust their time-consciousness and appreciate the emphasis on fellowship and warm spontaneity in their new fellowship.

Some cultural influences fall within the bounds of biblical principles, such as honoring others as image bearers or using our speech to bless others. Many cultural factors are matters of individual styles, habits, acquired learning, and personal beliefs that lie outside the line of God's truth. Because so many aspects of our thinking are shaped by culture and tradition, it's important to distinguish between truth and preferences.

Scripture provides us with examples of cultural factors that were important to God. For example, Miriam condemned Moses for marrying an Ethiopian woman, and God struck her with leprosy as punishment (Numbers 12). Philemon forgave Onesimus when his culture gave him legitimate reason to pursue the letter of the law. The good Samaritan had no reason to invest his time, money, and reputation on the stranger he found on the road between

Jerusalem and Jericho, yet love overwhelmed the pull of culture (Luke 10:27–37).

Have cultural influences shaped what you tell yourself is true about yourself, God, family members, relationships, and responsibilities to strangers and those in need? Have they influenced your ability to be a loving, compassionate, Christlike individual who relates at a heart level with others?

Does the cultural truth you embrace create conflict between you and others or help you love them more fully? Most importantly, has the cultural context of your life influenced you to think and act more like Jesus?

Sometimes our wounds speak most loudly, voicing shame and accusation, guilt and condemnation, bitterness and anger—trapping us and keeping us from growing in intimacy with God and others.

Voices of Friends

A friend of mine recently was sidelined by a barrage of painful circumstances: children in trouble with the law, loss of her husband's job, and devastating medical diagnoses. Frustrated and angry, she withdrew from Christian friends and turned to an online support group for counsel. The last time I spoke with her, she'd decided to move to the East Coast to meet a man she'd met in a chat room. Her online friends applauded her for pursuing happiness and leaving her "loser" husband and floundering children.

Other people can convince us to believe destructive things. The Israelites listened to fast-talking Absalom's selfish arguments and were seduced into rebelling against King David (2 Samuel 15–17). Jacob was convinced by his mother, Rebekah, to trick his father, Isaac, into giving him the blessing for the firstborn son that was meant for Esau, his older brother (Genesis 27).

At times the voices of close friends can drip with the poison of godless lies, even when they may have our best intentions at heart. Ultimately, we must be the gatekeepers of our minds.

Voices of Our Wounds

Sometimes our wounds speak most loudly, voicing shame and accusation, guilt and condemnation, bitterness and anger—trapping us and keeping us from growing in intimacy with God and others.

Lies about Ourselves

At the age of nineteen I was violently attacked by a man who'd raped more than forty women. Although I escaped through my bedroom window, I was emotionally and spiritually ravaged. For years I viewed myself as "damaged goods." It wasn't until years later that I began to recognize my victim mentality and manipulative mind-set.

Lies that spring from our wounds can take many forms:

I'm not good enough.
I'm ugly.
I'm worthless.
I'm flawed.
I've got to please everyone.
I'm a victim.
I'm useless.
I've got to be in control.
I've got to prove I'm better than everyone else.
I'm not strong enough to handle criticism.

The lies we tell ourselves about ourselves are some of our most powerful deceptions. They become blind spots in our thinking. But wounds don't always produce lies and negative self-talk. They can also be the impetus for growth.

The biblical character Joseph had the ultimate reasons to develop a victim mentality. His brothers plotted to kill him, finally settling on selling him into slavery (Genesis 37). Imagine the hatred and jealousy that prompted such a vicious act.

Certainly he had reason to slip into a "me-first" mind-set.

Yet we don't see Joseph shaking his fist at God, succumbing to bitterness or a victim mentality. Instead, he used his experiences to become a godly man—one who was used by God to save the lives of his family (Genesis 45).

When his brothers appeared before him years later, starving and begging for mercy, Joseph showed grace. He showed forgiveness. His confidence in God had penetrated his thinking, in spite of his circumstances.

When we're confident in God's protection, we feel freedom to extend protection and grace to others. Joseph experienced God's protection in the face of slavery, imprisonment, and abandonment, yet his gratitude compelled him to heap grace on his brothers. We can practically see the smile of expectancy on his face as he offers his family the same abundance God lavished on his life.

When we're confident in our position as God's image bearers, we're free to humbly serve, as Jesus did. As an image bearer of the Most High God, Joseph didn't need to prove his superiority over his brothers. He used his key position in Egypt as an opportunity to serve. His actions were deliberate. He chose to honor his family and restore broken relationships, in spite of his abuse at their hands.

When we're confident that God ensures our well-being, entrusts us with His power, and enables us through His Spirit, we live grace-driven lives. From the moment Joseph spotted his brothers, his actions were grace-driven. His purposes in setting up his youngest brother Benjamin were part of a plan that extended beyond providing his family with food, which alone would have been generous. After years of separation, Joseph's response was to devise a plan to restore his family to him by bringing Benjamin and eventually his father to him (Genesis 42:6–45:15).

Joseph's plan was devised to soften the hearts of those he loved and give them an opportunity to show whether or not they were men on the road to repentance. And Joseph's plan worked. When Judah faced the bitter truth that Benjamin would be forced to stay in Egypt and not allowed to return to his father, Judah offered himself as a slave in exchange for his youngest brother (Genesis 44:33–34).

Joseph became God's conduit of grace as the love of God coursed through him and new life and truth spilled out in the lives of his family.

Lies about Others

The pain of trauma and abuse can deafen us in the roar of lies about others.

Some people don't deserve to be forgiven.

They're no better than an animal.

They're so messed up, they really can't change anyway.

For years, I harbored hatred toward the rapist who'd assaulted me. I believed he was disgusting, vile, and didn't deserve forgiveness. I believed that a man who'd raped dozens of women didn't have much of a chance for redemption and a changed life.

My self-talk fed me lies straight from the pit of hell, and I didn't even feel the flames. It felt too soul-numbingly good to wallow in my bitterness.

In our woundedness, we often strip others of their rightful place at the foot of the cross beside us. But in our woundedness we must be ruthless in examining our motives and self-talk.

Do we feel a surge of self-satisfaction as we contemplate the sin of others or the humiliation of someone we disdain?

Do we compare ourselves with others to inflate our pride?

Do we use words that diminish human dignity and value

—racial slurs, sexist terms, cultural slams, political insults?

Do our thoughts drift to conversations, comebacks, rebuttals, defenses regarding situations with those who've wounded us?

Unhealed wounds fester. But Joseph's words and actions in Genesis chapter 39, 42, and 43 reveal he'd experienced the power of forgiveness to say no to the seduction of sin.

He flat-out refused Mrs. Potiphar's repeated attempts to seduce him.

He didn't mull it over long enough to rationalize. He simply slapped down her invitation for sex with the truth—his master had been good to him, and to think about disloyalty was sin against both him and God (Genesis 39:9).

When Joseph's straightforward refusal to Potiphar's wife didn't work, he cut off contact with her (Genesis 39:11).

When cutting off contact didn't work, he ran (Genesis 39:15).

Joseph's actions proved the power of his self-talk. Other people's interests came first—God's, his boss's, his brothers', even Potiphar's wife's as he refused to use her to his advantage. Even after years of imprisonment, when he was given the opportunity to protect himself and seek power and position by interpreting Pharaoh's dream by his own ability, Joseph used his circumstances to point his hands toward heaven and glorify God.

> *"I cannot do it [interpret the dream]," Joseph replied to Pharaoh, "but God will give Pharaoh the answer he desires."*
>
> —Genesis 41:16

In the face of abandonment, abuse, accusation, betrayal, and blackmailing, Joseph refused to allow bitter self-talk to warp his view of God. Instead, his faith was strengthened, and he chose to see himself as an instrument to carry out God's work of blessing (Genesis 45:4–11).

Lies about God

When God allows pain to touch us, our first response is often to question His character and doubt His love. Like Eve, we may doubt that a God who would withhold good things could really be the good God He pretends to be.

We wrap our arms around our pain-wracked baby in a pediatric unit and wonder how God could be good.

We turn away from the cancer-ravaged body of our husband and wonder how a loving God could allow a thirty-five-year-old mother to face life as a widow.

We listen to our daughter's broken voice on the phone as she pours out details of her husband's physical abuse and wonder if our pleas for her protection have been in vain.

Is God really . . .

A God we can trust, who is who He says He is, a God who really loves us?

Self-talk rises up from the wound, where sting penetrates the superficial and makes its way to bone and blood and soul. And our image of God becomes a reflection of our doubt and disillusionment, our bitterness and blame.

Yet Joseph didn't fall into the trap of the blame game. His brothers abused him, abandoned him, and sold him into slavery, and he didn't blame God. He was set up by Potiphar's wife, and he didn't blame God. The chief cupbearer didn't make good on his promise to remember Joseph to Pharaoh, and he didn't blame God. No matter what life handed him, Joseph refused to allow accusations about the character of God to get a grip on his thought life. Instead, we see him using every opportunity to remind people around him that God was responsible for the good that had come into his life (Genesis 39:9; 40:8; 41:15–16, 25b, 28a, 32b, 51–52; 45:4–8).

In spite of repeated wounding, Joseph found rest in the character of God. He was not a pawn but a servant of God sent ahead for a purpose. His pain was redeemed. What had appeared to be chaos was woven together in a tapestry that would change the course of history.

We, too, are promised eternal purpose and discernment in difficult times. The example of the apostle Paul points the way.

Self-talk rises up from the wound, where sting penetrates the superficial and makes its way to bone and blood and soul.

TUNING OUT THE DIN

If anyone in Scripture worked to tame the voices of his self-talk, it was the apostle Paul. Until his conversion to faith in Christ, he'd spent a lifetime feeding his self-righteous ego and convincing himself he was doing it for the sake of truth. In Philippians 3:4, he describes his former pride as "confidence in the flesh," then lists his accomplishments in verses 5 and 6 to demonstrate that, according to his critics' standards, he had amazing religious and cultural credentials.

First of all, Paul cited his cultural heritage as a pure-blooded Jew and son of two Hebrew parents, which was demonstrated by his circumcision on the eighth day. Paul could trace his Jewish lineage back to Abraham (2 Corinthians 11:22). Galatians 1:13–14 tells us that, due in part to the influence of his education, Paul intensely persecuted followers of Jesus in his younger years. Paul was most likely a type A personality, driven to advance as a Pharisee in Judaism. He burned to rise above the rest, and along the way, he convinced himself that persecuting the church was a logical way to demonstrate his devotion to his faith.

I too was convinced that I ought to do all that was possible to oppose the name of Jesus of Nazareth. And that is just what I did in Jerusalem. On the authority of the chief priests I put many of the saints in prison, and when they were put to death, I cast my vote against them.

—ACTS 26:9

Beyond his heritage, Paul chose to immerse himself in the Jewish faith even further by becoming a Pharisee, the strictest sect among the Jews, which layered even more rules and regulations over the Law. And in his drive to prove himself a righteous man, Paul persecuted the church relentlessly. And if that weren't enough, he devoted himself to legalistic works.

As we read Paul's account of his former life, we can almost hear the mind of the "old" Paul at work:

In a world where birth and social standing meant everything, I had a pedigree that ranked above all others. But no one worked harder than I did to advance themselves among the leaders in the religious world. It was my goal to gain a position of influence and power—even if I had to abuse power and people to do it. And I managed to tell myself I was doing it all to the glory of God.

Paul's zeal to prove his religious devotion had made him a slave to his self-interests as he'd fought to protect religious tradition, to position himself, to promote his agenda, and to procure power. But in spite of his hard-fought battle to be a good man, he finally faced the truth—no matter how hard he tried to gain righteousness on his own, he was destined to fail.

For I have the desire to do what is good, but I cannot carry it out. For what I do is not the good I want to do; no, the evil I do not want to do—this I keep on doing.

—ROMANS 7:18b–19

So how did Paul, despite his background of oppressing believers, use the power of self-talk to move forward in his faith, even assuming a leadership role in the church, rather than allowing the past to bury him in doubt and disgrace?

CONSIDERING, WANTING, FORGETTING, AND STRAINING

Voices of shame and accusation could have destroyed Paul's ministry before it ever began. Imagine living with the reality that you were responsible for the persecution, torture, and death of fellow Christians. It would be easy for self-talk to drive you to despair. Fellow believers would have every earthly reason to despise you and view you as an enemy. Yet after Paul became a believer in Jesus, he didn't see himself as a failure or wallow in self-pity. He refused to look back at his former life and focused on what he'd gained and his new calling. He understood the power of considering.

Considering

> *But whatever was to my profit I now consider loss for the sake of Christ. What is more, I consider everything a loss compared to the surpassing greatness of knowing Christ Jesus my Lord, for whose sake I have lost all things. I consider them rubbish, that I may gain Christ and be found in him, not having a righteousness of my own that comes from the law, but that which is through faith in Christ—the righteousness that comes from God and is by faith. I want to know Christ and the power of his resurrection and the fellowship of sharing in his sufferings.*
>
> —PHILIPPIANS 3:7–10

The greatness of knowing Christ redeemed Paul's past spiritually, but Paul still *chose to consider* everything from a new perspective because of his relationship with Christ. Considering is an action requiring self-talk and meditation. It means to "think through or reflect upon" and means we weigh options, pros and cons, consequences, and outcomes. Paul made life-altering choices after he met Jesus on the Damascus Road (Acts 9). Would he continue to put his confidence in his heritage and his own efforts, or in Jesus Christ, a man he'd believed to be dead but who'd spoken directly to him with a voice that emanated from a holy strobe light?

Suddenly Paul's world was turned upside down as he faced what that voice had told him. Was Jesus really who He claimed to be—God's Son who'd died to pay the price for his sins? If it was all true, how would his life have to change?

The account of Paul's conversion in Acts chapter 9 is silent regarding his inner struggle. We aren't allowed to see his raw emotion, his rationalization, and the final crushing blow as his spirit crumpled under the weight of his sin. But we do see the Paul who emerges—a man zealously devoted to Christ as everything precious to him in his former life is transformed into rubbish before his eyes (Philippians 3:8). A new devotion replaces the old—an all-consuming passion for Jesus that makes Paul's former zeal for legalistic Judaism pale into the merest of shadows.

Wanting

A second key to Paul's power over his self-talk came in his pure passion, in *wanting to know Christ.*

> *I want to know Christ and the power of his resurrection and the fellowship of sharing in his sufferings, becoming like him in his death.*
>
> —PHILIPPIANS 3:10–11

Paul was willing and ready, first of all, to associate himself with Jesus' physical suffering as His representative. But he was also expressing his desire to be conformed to the inward character of Jesus—to be crucified and brought to life as a new man from the inside out.

Paul's passion to be like Jesus made it possible for him to face imprisonment, beating, deprivation, and persecution with an attitude of sacrifice and self-denial. His passion and longing to be like Christ transformed his self-talk and gave him the ability to claim his position as a son of God, to think and act like a servant, and to endure suffering as a soldier.

Forgetting

Another key in Paul's power over his self-talk was his decision to *forget what was behind.*

> *Forgetting what is behind and straining toward what is ahead.*
>
> —Philippians 3:13

Paul refused to follow the voices from his past—shame, accusation, blame, guilt, failure, abandonment, lost dreams, broken friendships. But he also didn't say he *had forgotten* the things that were behind—he was in the process of *forgetting* them. Even Paul couldn't simply eradicate the power of his past and transform his self-talk in one life-changing moment. Forgetting is a process of diminishment of influence, of fading.

As paradoxical as it may sound, forgetting of the sort Paul mentions in this passage is an act of the will. It requires placement of thought. It asks the forgetter to look to what lies ahead, instead of the hurts of the past. This type of forgetting is experienced by mothers who've known the pain of labor and delivery and yet choose to conceive again for the love of a child. In the forgetting and the releasing of our old man, the Spirit makes way for new life. But Paul knew that forgetting was only the starting point to "the surpassing greatness of knowing Christ." He also knew that to know Christ would require an act of determination.

Straining

At the same moment Paul was committed to forgetting his former accomplishments, he was also *straining* toward what God had set before him—his calling in Jesus. The word used in this passage comes from a Greek athletic term that describes a runner whose eyes draw his hand forward, and his hand pulls his entire body forward.[7]

Those of us who saw 2008 Olympic swimmer Michael Phelps compete in the 100 meter butterfly saw a perfect portrayal of this term. As Mark laid his body out for the final strokes toward the wall with Serbian swimmer Milorad Cavic in the next lane, it appeared that Cavic had the lead. But straining with every muscle in his body, Phelps stretched into the final push to the wall and won the gold medal with a victory of only .01 of a second.

Straining doesn't come without effort or cost. It doesn't come without pain or struggle. But the gleam reflecting from the prize casts a shadow over things of this world as we follow our calling in Christ Jesus and the promise that we will be conformed to His character. God has promised to give us the very mind of Christ: love, joy, peace, long-suffering, gentleness, goodness, faith, humility, patience. But we must be committed to engaging our muscles—in loving the unlovely and acting with humility in the face of arrogance, in choosing joy in sorrow and long-suffering in the face of persecution, in expressing gentleness in the presence of violence and good in the face of evil, in standing as instruments of peace in conflict and finding patience in the midst of turbulence.

We live in a world of chaos. The voices of family, friends, culture, tradition, and wounds pull at us. We struggle to hear the Spirit of God in the din.

The apostle Paul assures us we strive for an achievable prize, to find fellowship with a knowable God.

Considering, wanting, forgetting, straining—these key principles draw us forward in our growth in Christ. As we tune out the clamor of life and turn our hearts to the voice of the Spirit, a growing desire overtakes our thoughts—to sit at the table and bask in the presence of the One we love.

SOUL SEARCH
Breaking the Silence

- What aspects of your "family culture" influence your self-talk in a positive, biblical way? Name specific areas and describe how your thinking has influenced your living out the double love command in your relationship with God and your relationships with others.
- What aspects of your "family culture" influence your self-talk with negative nonbiblical thinking? Describe how this thinking has blocked your relationship with God and with others.
- How do the voices of friends influence your self-talk, both positively and negatively?
- How have your wounds influenced your self-talk? What messages have they shaped about your value and worth or your view of others or God?
- Where do you struggle with "forgetting what is behind"? How does your self-talk affect you in this area? What steps have you taken to make your forgetting a deliberate process?

FACING THE SEDUCTION
Listening to the Spirit and the Word

1. Imagine you're Joseph. How did his self-talk contribute to the healing of his relationships with his family? Think through the following Scripture passages as possible applications.

Matthew 6:12–14 Ephesians 4:31–32
Psalm 103

2. Paul states that he considered everything loss compared to knowing Jesus. His life was tough. He was constantly on the move and was shipwrecked, imprisoned, and persecuted. What kind of self-talk would you expect from him as he faced his trials? Does this seem like something that's really possible when you're facing great loss?
3. What does "straining toward what is ahead" look like in your self-talk? How are you pressing forward to trust Jesus more, to know Him better, to listen to the voice of the Spirit? Consider meditating on the following passages.

   1 John 2:5, 15, 17
   1 John 3:1, 6, 16, 18–22
   1 John 5:1–5

4. See appendix 9 for an additional resource on *Listening to Your Self-Talk in the Clamor of Life.*

RESPONDING FROM THE HEART
Prayer

Father God, Your Word tells me that grace and peace are mine in abundance through knowledge of You and of Jesus. His divine power has given me everything I need for life and godliness through knowledge of Him who called us by His own glory and goodness. Through these He has given us His very great and precious promises so that through them I may participate in the divine nature and escape the corruption in the world caused by evil desires.

For this reason, Father, I'm making every effort to add to my faith, goodness; and to goodness, knowledge; and to knowledge, self-control; and to self-control, perseverance; and to perseverance, godliness; and to godliness, brotherly kindness; and to brotherly kindness, love. If I possess these qualities in increasing measures, they will keep me from being ineffective and unproductive in my knowledge of my Lord Jesus (2 Peter 1:2–8).

Father, I am beloved in You, and nothing can separate me from Your love. Your Spirit is healing the broken places in me. You have given me all I need to live a godly life. Free me from a spirit of fear of my past, of my failures, of the future, of man. Expose the lies in my heart and mind and allow me to hear Your Spirit. Fulfill Your every purpose in my life, and pour out the joy that is mine as Your child. Amen.

CHAPTER 8

CRANKING UP *the Volume:*

Learning to Listen

Much silence makes a powerful noise.

—AFRICAN PROVERB

We've all heard it a thousand times. Okay, maybe three or four—a sermon on the double love command, that passage in Matthew 22 where we're told to love God with all our heart, soul, and mind, and our neighbor as ourselves.

And we yawn. We think we get it.

Love God a lot. Love people a lot—even the ones we'd rather see staked out on a giant anthill.

Like the luggage handler who pawed through our suitcase and stole Grandma's locket.

Or the ex-husband who poisons our name when he has the kids.

Even the caregiver who left a bruise on our mother's arm. People who make forgiveness hard to swallow.

Love all of them out of the overflow of God's enormous love for us. Love them as lavishly and openhandedly as we crave to be loved ourselves. As openhandedly as God forgave us—without holding back a second thought or glimmer of regret.

I'd heard the double love command preached plenty of times in my nearly fifty years of dribbling my love into the world from a thimble. One sermon had sounded pretty much like the next until the day I heard Louie preach on loving the way God loves. Louie pastors the church Dan and I joined after moving back to Michigan from Iowa, and two and a half minutes into his sermon that morning, I was suddenly afraid. Something in me knew I was about to be soul-smacked, and my life would never be the same.

Louie is a godly and gifted soul-smacker. He has a Spirit-filled way of whacking those blessed enough to sit under his teaching upside the heart, sending us running into the arms of Jesus. Even when he preaches on passages I've heard explained a dozen times, I see God with fresh eyes. Most Sundays in those first months, I'd cry, take soggy notes, and float to my car awakened to God's love for me like a moonstruck teenager.

Louie's sermon on the double love command switched on a spotlight in my soul. For the first time, I could see the self-centered nature that drove me—sinful habits, selfish attitudes, and patterns of responding that had become so ingrained in me that I'd tuned them out. It wasn't a pretty picture, but it was a picture I needed to see.

But superimposed over the vivid image of my needy soul was the brilliant reality of the Spirit of God at work in my heart.

He had not abandoned me. He wanted to change me.

But God couldn't begin the work of surgery unless I first saw my need and submitted to His hands.

I left church that day with a prayer pressing on my heart—"Show me what I need to see about myself so You can change me, Lord."

As the weeks passed, God began to answer that prayer. He showed me I could begin to understand my motives if I would take the time to stop, look, and listen to myself *before, as,* and *after* I spoke and acted. Since I'm a consummate interrupter and conversation hog, I knew this would be hard. But even admitting this to myself gave me a starting point.

Weeks passed, and I worked to begin each day by "pre-setting" my thinking to be a videographer of my thoughts. I discovered it was possible to pull myself away from my self-talk like an observer and "listen in" on my thinking. As many times as possible throughout the day, I'd pull myself into my videographer mind-set and listen in on where my self-talk took me—as I was driving, taking my seat in church, preparing for a meeting, starting the day.

I slipped into my educator's role and became a student of myself. I picked up a notebook and pen, settled back, and asked God to help me hear the voices that chattered inside my soul—mine, His, and the Enemy's.

I had no idea what I was in for.

SITTIN' DOWN AND SHUTTIN' UP

Not far into my journey, the Spirit of God put a megaphone to my ear and blasted a message.

"Sit down and be still. How can you hear what I've got to say if you're filling all the airtime?"

Up to this point in my life, my devotional time hadn't included silence. In my head, silence was not golden—it was filled with random thoughts: grocery lists, guilt about not flossing, questions about where all the unmated socks have run off to, and snippets of songs that had lodged in my head from last week.

But God is patient—even with deranged writers. Day after day, I heard the Spirit of God encouraging me.

"You can do this, Shelly. Just sit and be still in My presence and listen."

And so instead of yammering away with my list of "please bless-es" in my devotions, I read Scripture and listened. I waited. I asked God to speak and use His Word to show me what I needed to see. From the very first day, truth began to pop off the pages of the Bible faster than a blazing bag of Jiffy Pop.

Conversations and scenarios rolled through my mind, and one tiny explosion of truth at a time, I saw what I hadn't seen before.

Controlling, distrustful motives.

A demanding, self-serving spirit.

Manipulative, grasping goals.

And I saw God's arms flung wide with grace to welcome me as my spirit broke in sorrow and repentance.

In an instant I saw myself free, forgiven, and complete in Jesus, arrayed in His righteousness.

I saw myself unleashed to move forward and be who God created me to be as His dear daughter.

Instead of feeling overwhelmed with guilt, I felt a rush of excitement. God was talking to me, moving in me, changing me. It took days for that magnificent truth to sink in. He wanted to revolutionize my life, and His presence would take me where He needed me to go. Every moment of every day offered me the potential for breaking free from the slavery of old habits and patterns.

In the days that followed, I ripped through the pages of my Bible to see what God had to say to me. He was talking, and I was listening.

It felt like I'd won some amazing kind of lottery. I bought a new notebook for Louie's sermon notes, and Dan and I arrived early every Sunday to stake out our claim in the fifth row, left-hand side, center row. Heaven help the person who tried to take our seats. Week after week, God's Word hit me between the eyes, and the pain never felt so sweet. I'd never realized I was such a mess, and I'd never felt so amazed by the love of God that was poured out to make me more like His Son.

It was the best of times, and it was the worst of times. It still is. But you'll never know the best of times in Jesus until you've seen your heart at its worst.

TAKIN' IT TO THE STREETS

My spiritual growth spurt seemed easy until a second Sunday—weeks later—when Louie preached on the double love command,

and a familiar face popped up in front of my eyes. Someone I was polite to, gracious to, someone I even went out of my way to be kind to. Someone I'd tried to love. At least that's what I'd always told myself.

And it wasn't as if this person made it easy for people to be around her. Even her Christian friends rolled their eyes and wagged their heads so much when they talked about her that they looked like bobble-head dolls. They were experts at the thinly veiled disrespect we all practice—subtle facial expressions, sighs, shakes of the head, a few cautious phrases tossed in here and there to test the waters of shared disdain. Then the occasional tantalizing statement of judgment thrown into the discussion like a piece of meat on stick, only to be quickly withdrawn if too many people swept in to grab it up.

(After all, it wasn't spiritual to gossip.)

I'd been doing well studying my self-talk, meditating, discovering long-concealed motives. But suddenly the nagging suspicion that I wasn't loving this friend well grew from an occasional whisper to a full-blown shout, even as I rationalized that I was doing a better job than everyone else I chose to compare myself with. Deep down, I knew I was afraid. I didn't want to take risks. I didn't want to rebuke gossip. I didn't want to talk to my friend about her own caustic behavior. I was unwilling to love her as a friend deserved to be loved. I was a fraud.

The Spirit of God faced me with my hypocrisy in the fifth row, left-hand side, center seat as I sat with my pen hovering over my notebook.

What would it mean to really love this woman God had placed in my life?

Had I ever really tried to love anyone as myself?

A DAY IN THE LIFE OF A HYPOCRITE

The following day I made my choice as I headed out the door to work. I'd hone in on my motives and self-talk in my interactions with my friend. In about a minute and a half I'd figured out that up to this point, my motives had often been superficial—to keep from ruffling her feathers and serve my own selfish agenda at work.

But living out the double love command would mean trying to love her as I wanted to be loved myself. I knew it would be hard, that I'd have to analyze my self-talk honestly as I moved through my day. I'd have to talk less and listen to myself more and evaluate my motives and goals along the way.

It seemed easy enough. But it would only have been easy if I'd stayed home and pulled the covers over my head.

I didn't expect the fun to begin before my car hit the first stop sign on the way to work, and I began thinking about the change I was actually trying to make.

So what would it mean for me to really love someone the way I want my friends to love me? What do I value in a friend?

I want friends who are willing to do tough things, sacrificial things. Friends who stand up for me, even when it costs them something. I want friends who love unconditionally and forgive with an open heart. Friends who call out a vision for who God wants me to become and see beyond my flaws. I want friends who stick beside me in the hard times and lift me out of the mud and clean me up when I land in the gutter. Friends who rejoice when I rejoice and cry when I cry. And I want friends who are willing to look me in the face and tell me the hard things no one else is willing to say.

And are you that kind of friend to this woman?

No. It would be risky. She's volatile. She has power. There are too many ways it could end up hurting me. Why can't being polite and nice be enough—maybe working my way up to putting my foot down on the gossip? Why should "loving as myself" mean I have to get tangled up in her life? She has other friends for that. Nothing in the Bible says I'm responsible for being best friends with everybody I meet.

Copping out already? Or is the truth that you don't genuinely love her at all or even like her very much—except for the times you've been willing to use your relationship to make yourself look good or latch on to power?

I don't think I like where you're going with this.

How about to your motives? Have you seen any manipulation, any hypocrisy—looking out for yourself but making it look like you were doing the right thing on the surface? When people were gossiping the other day, did you step in and suggest it might be hurtful? Did you even have the courage to walk away? Or did you just stand there and convince yourself you were spiritual because you didn't actually throw down the judgmental statement that was rolling around in your brain? That's some kind of weird inside-out pride you've got going on.

Okay, I've been trying to love this person for three whole minutes, and I've already fallen flat on my face.

So get back up. What would it mean to really love her today the way you think Jesus would do it? To walk into a room, forget about yourself, and focus on her?

But she's not even a close friend. And what about her prickly personality—the bitterness and criticism she flings around that makes her so hard to love? I'm not going to do her any good if I slather love all over her and let her get away with bashing people.

Did Jesus waste His time loving people who were less than lovely? And let's count the times you've prayed for her. Not like a Pharisee, with that hint of disdain tingeing your words. Do you feel burdened for her? Or just annoyed because you're convinced you're a better Christian than she is?

Okay, so I really don't pray for her much, and when I do, I've got a lot of pride sloshing around. And I spend a lot of time being annoyed and comparing her to myself. So maybe the point of all this is that I need to pray for me because I'm so selfish. I guess I don't have a clue what loving really looks like, and I need to figure out if I'm willing to love with my heart, soul, and strength and risk paying the price. I know this woman's hurt a lot of people. Really loving her would mean laying down my rights and my fear. It would mean a lot more mucking around in my motives, and I've seen enough in a fifteen-minute drive to work to make me see that really loving means giving up everything.

The conversation played out in my head the entire day . . . for months as I kept the camera rolling on my thoughts and a notebook in my purse. I began to see patterns emerge in my relationship with my friend and in my thinking in general. I found myself drawn toward selfish decisions motivated by selfish goals. I watched myself go into meetings and smile sweetly while inside my head I heaped judgment and criticism on others in the room. I manipulated conversations and situations to my advantage. And more than once, I turned away from opportunities to speak lovingly to my friend about her caustic criticism of others.

With revelation comes freedom. Each nudge of the Holy Spirit redirected my self-talk to the Father as I ran to Him in prayer.

Observing my attitudes and self-talk was exhausting work, and I developed a love/hate relationship with my notebook. But day after day, the Spirit of God revealed more of my heart with each new revelation. And with each new revelation, my thoughts and my actions changed.

With revelation comes freedom. Each nudge of the Holy Spirit redirected my self-talk to the Father as I ran to Him in prayer. I began to see a new cycle emerge in my life—sensitivity to the Spirit, conviction of sin, conversation with God, freedom and renewal, changed behavior. One thought at a time, one day at a time, my mind was being renewed, and I was loving God more and loving others better.

Those months and the journey since have shown me that I'm a stinky sinner with a selfish heart, but Jesus gave His life so sin's stench doesn't have to hang off me. Because of Jesus, I can bear the sweet aroma of a redeemed life. I can learn to think like Him and act like Him. And I can learn to love like Him—freely, exuberantly, lavishly.

STEPS TOWARD REDEEMING OUR SELF-TALK

My prayer since those first days of hearing the sin-twisted whispers of my self-talk was for God to crank up the volume so His Holy Spirit could drop me to my knees with a smack to my head and my heart. I cannot be changed until I first understand how desperately I need to be changed. When I first realized that my mind was a battleground, and I was at war with myself for my thoughts, will, emotions, and God's purposes to be carried out in my life, I made up my mind to study my self-talk. I asked God to turn up the volume so I could hear the voices, gain wisdom and discernment, and wrestle them to defeat in areas where I'd given them power over my life.

My first request was to ask God to **reveal my hidden, ungodly spiritual motives**. I knew that among the good things in my heart, I'd tucked away hidden agendas, and I asked God to show me where my self-talk conflicted with biblical thinking and areas where my rationalization of entitlement had influenced my attitudes and life choices:

- Attitudes of entitlement—in my marriage, my family, my friendships, my work relationships
- Ungodly motives and goals
- Unloving and unbiblical ways I responded to people I didn't like
- Unloving and unbiblical ways I responded to circumstances I didn't like—frustrations, discouragement, annoyances, disappointment, betrayal, rejection
- The self-deceiving arguments and excuses I'd erected
- Areas where my thinking ran contrary to biblical truth

It was an intimidating list, and as I prayed, I waited for a celestial Mack truck to back up to my yard and dump a load of guilt and despair over my soul. But something far more astounding happened.

God reminded me of His plan to grow me into the woman He'd created me to be. He overwhelmed me with a reminder of His inescapable, all-surpassing love. He adored me. I was His precious daughter. I wasn't a failure and didn't need to hang my head in shame. He was thrilled that I wanted to love Him more, and He'd already supplied everything I needed to grow into my calling in Jesus. His riches were mine, and I claimed Ephesians 1:18–19: "I pray also that the eyes of your heart may be enlightened in order that you may know the hope to which he has called you, the riches of his glorious inheritance in the saints, and his incomparably great power for us who believe."

My second priority was to **continue to journal.** I purchased a notebook large enough to record detail but small enough to keep in my purse because self-talk happens everywhere, and where self-talk happens . . .

- jealousy happens.
- envy happens.
- lust happens.
- resentment happens.
- anger happens.

Whispers of entitlement call to us a hundred times a day—telling us we have a right to rage, to indulge in pride, to gorge on resentment, to criticize and complain, to shove our way to the front of the line. Some mornings my feet don't hit the floor before a complaining spirit begins sniping in my head, telling me to dump my frustrations on Dan. At times one eye is barely opened before I have to begin the work of asking, *Where did this lousy attitude come from? What am I telling myself I'm entitled to, and is what I believe really the truth? Am I depending on God or relying on people to come through for me instead?* On bad days, when I've thought about giving in and giving up, I've thought about wearing a sign around my neck: *Warning: Child of God Under Construction—Slow Learner.*

Because I was trying to negotiate my way through a lifetime of misplaced motives and unexplored self-talk, I found the help of a good Christian counselor. Through my church, I was blessed to have access to a qualified counselor, and I would have been foolish to have wasted an opportunity to enlist Gary's wisdom. He helped me recognize blind spots in my thinking and understand the victim mentality that had held me captive most of my life. He provided accountability, balance, and encouragement. He grieved with me over my failures and applauded my victories. He helped Dan and me work through toxic patterns of relating, and we saw our marriage revitalized. Most important, he helped me think biblically.

Proverbs 13:10 tell us that "wisdom is found in those who take advice," and verse 20 states that "he who walks with the wise grows wise." The counsel, support, and wisdom of godly mentors and accountability partners is invaluable as we try to break free from patterns of thinking that have kept us in bondage and look for a healthier understanding of ourselves. Their prayer, support, and perspective may be the nourishment we need to bring fresh growth to our journey.

LOOKING FROM THE OUTSIDE, IN

A few days ago Dan and I were tooling down the road together, and Something Stupid bubbled up inside me—an angry, entitled spirit. As I recall, Dan was doing something highly offensive. He wasn't breathing correctly.

Really.

I hate it when he does that.

I toyed with my desire to flick a look, to sigh, to fling a one-liner.

In that split second, I was faced with a choice. Step into the double love command and the beauty of God's vision for me, or step into the demanding spirit calling to me.

He inhaled again in his rhythmic, in-and-out pattern that makes my eyes spin.

But I hunkered down. I shut my mouth, cranked up my self-talk and asked myself the tough questions.

Why am I such a control freak that I have to correct even the breathing of the man I love?

By the time our car hit the driveway, I knew I had no right to my frustration. I dropped the attitude and stepped into the double love command. I made a choice.

Love God.

Love Dan the way I want to be loved.

Pry my fingers off my feeling of entitlement and let it fall back into the flames of hell.

It seemed like a small victory, but, of course, that's not really true. I'd chosen a daughter's act of love for her Father.

Deliberate.

Purposeful.

An act of worship.

I think, perhaps, the angels danced.

SOUL SEARCH
Breaking the Silence

- What sinful habits, behaviors, rationalizations, and patterns of responding to people do you suspect you've "tuned out" over the years? Do you have the courage to ask a few trusted, spiritually discerning friends about their observations in these areas?
- How would you rate yourself at loving God with your heart, soul, and mind? At loving others? At loving those who annoy you or who've abused you?
- Over the past few years, how aware have you been of the battles for truth in your mind—everyday battles for your emotions, choices, attitudes? What do you think has contributed to your awareness or lack of awareness?

Facing the Seduction
Listening to the Spirit and the Word

1. Get a notebook and begin praying and asking God to reveal truth to you in the following areas:
    - Attitudes of entitlement
    - Ungodly motives and goals
    - Unloving and unbiblical ways you respond to people you don't like
    - Unloving and unbiblical ways you respond to circumstances you don't like—frustrations, discouragement, annoyances, disappointment, betrayal, rejection
    - Arguments and excuses you've deceived yourself with for years
    - Areas where your thinking runs contrary to biblical truth
    - How to begin to change and grow into the godly woman God wants you to become

2. Practice silence and become a videographer. Step back from your life and listen in to what you're saying. Is it biblical, or is it just what you want to hear?
3. Consider the help of a biblical counselor, godly mentor, or accountability partner as you "turn up the voices." You're sure to have spiritual opposition as you begin this journey, and you'll need encouragement and cheerleading along the way. You might want to consider a Bible study with others so you can share insights together.

RESPONDING FROM THE HEART
Prayer

Father, give me the courage to look at my attitudes, my motives, and my self-talk, and give me the wisdom to see myself through Your eyes. Every experience in my life is an opportunity to experience Your faithfulness and Your provision, and so often I fail to see things that way. You bring problems into my life so I can access Your deep wisdom and grow in intimacy with You. More than anything, You want me to be like Jesus, and every problem and challenge I face is an opportunity to grow to be more like Him if I'm just willing to listen to the moving of Your Spirit and step forward in faith. Help me see that this life isn't about reaching for what I want but releasing all that I have to You.

Help me realize that other people aren't here to solve my problems. Help me search out Your wisdom. Give me perseverance to dig into Your Word for the precious truth You've given me. Give me endurance and perseverance to seek Your solutions instead of the quick and easy ones I so often want. Help me recognize thinking that buys into the Enemy's lies. Give me the mind of Christ and His perspective on my circumstances and problems. May I have the desire to embrace His solutions in spite of the cost and to do it with joy, knowing I'm fulfilling my destiny as Your precious child. Amen.

CHAPTER 9

WHODA THOUGHT *Fruit Could Be So Sweet?*

Transforming Truths about Our Self-Talk

One is wise to cultivate the tree that bears fruit in our soul.

—HENRY DAVID THOREAU

From the moment I first saw the neat brick and cedar ranch, I claimed it as our new Michigan home. And I knew it would be the scene of another of my murders.

As I stood in the front yard among the rosebushes after the walk-through, I felt the first stab of guilt. I could envision the death that was to come.

And such a waste.

It was obvious the former owners had maintained the house with devotion. Their meticulous care showed in details of craftsmanship and tasteful choices, nowhere as visibly as in their gardenlike yard.

And they'd sold the fruit of their labors, the work of their hands, to a botanical axe murderer.

By way of explanation, I have never killed with deliberation. But I have been responsible for accidental homicide by means of over-hydration, over-fertilization, and memory loss. All manner of flora have fallen dead at my feet.

The heartiest of cacti.

The sturdiest of evergreens.

The pinkest of roses.

I've killed plants my friends swore could be shoved under a bed and watered every other month during leap years. But not so. Within days even aloe was dead on the counter beside my microwave.

I have never felt the slightest devotion to plants, unless perhaps they were mashed potatoes. I forget them entirely and then, out of guilt, douse them with buckets of water. This cycle is typically followed by the "plucking of dead leaves" phase, repeated abandonings and dousings with guilt-water, and the inevitable trip to the trash can.

I have certainly never known what it means to love my plants with my heart, soul, and mind. I've never mustered even faint affection for them.

Except for one.

When our daughter, Jessica, was eleven years old, her best friend Kirk, who was also eleven, died in a tragic accident. Kirk's parents were our dear friends and gave us a corn plant from one of his memorials.

Suddenly, one plant had my undivided attention—"Kirk's plant." I watered it. I repotted, dusted, and rotated it. When we moved to a new home, it moved. I doted on my plant until it grew to be so large that it vied for space with our Christmas tree.

After forty years as botanical assassin, I'd fallen in love with a corn plant. And why? Because I loved Kirk. Suddenly my neglectful spirit had become intentional and nurturing because I was reminded how much we cherished the child we missed so dearly.

For the first time, I tended a plant with my heart. I did it for the sake of love.

FEEDING OUR PASSION

What we fail to feed ultimately dies of starvation. Even passions must be fed, or they die. Søren Kirkegaard has said, "Our life always expresses the results of our dominant thoughts." The day the serpent approached Eve in the garden of Eden, her actions revealed the roots of a soul parched by ingratitude and lack of reverence for God. Romans 1:21 describes her heart:

> *For although [Eve] knew God, [she] neither glorified him as God nor gave thanks to him, but [her] thinking became futile and [her] foolish [heart was darkened].*

While this passage is speaking about God's indictment on the sins of the world, Eve initiated the process in the book of Genesis with a few flickering thoughts. In her brief interchange with the serpent, she glanced away from the face of her Lord and into Satan's warped reflection of reality. In that moment . . .

Gratitude was swallowed up by a grasping spirit.

Reverence rotted into skepticism, and Eve's true identity was swallowed by artifice, striving, and guilt.

Tending our passion for God is the most important work we will ever be called to do. Waning passion for God was the key to Israel's lost blessings in the Old Testament. Passion for Jesus and God's kingdom purposes drove the apostles' ministries and the spread of the New Testament church in the face of fierce persecution. Passion for the Father and His mission define Jesus' character and should ignite the core of our being.

Blaise Pascal has said, "Happiness is neither outside us nor inside us; it is in God, both outside and inside us." So how do we tend our souls and feed our passion for God? How do we water roots of gratitude and cultivate a spirit that listens for His voice?

Yesterday I went to my friend Sally's funeral. She died of colon cancer at the age of fifty-six after a ten-month struggle that played out in a doxology of praise. Her words in the first days of her diagnosis were "I don't want to waste this."

Sally believed that each moment of her life had been marked out with eternal destiny, had been charged with Spirit-filled power, and came hardwired to the purposes of the Father. She lived with full expectancy that every thought and every breath were linked to His. No matter where life took her, she couldn't escape His loving reach. Sally gloried in that knowledge until her dying breath. Her final words—"No regrets."

WHODA THOUGHT FRUIT COULD BE SO SWEET?

One of the most amazing things about our self-talk is our power to deceive ourselves into thinking preposterous things.

Take, for instance, the idea that God doesn't hear what's going on inside our heads. That maybe He's too busy diverting comets from colliding with Earth or He's sidetracked by corruption in Hollywood or Washington or in the life of that guy in the pew in front of us.

But the simple, bone-chilling truth is that God hears everything we mutter to ourselves in the privacy of our thoughts—the good, the bad, the downright scandalous.

Chew on that for a moment. Where have your thoughts taken you today?

God is listening. His Holy Spirit lives in us. But He hasn't taken up residence inside us because He's on a secret wire-tapping mission. He lives within us because He desires to "tabernacle" in us—to make our bodies, souls, and spirits His very Holy of Holies. Theologian Abraham Kuyper states, "Every day of our lives we know fellowship with [God], that his voice sounds in our lives as regularly as the ticking of the mantle clock, that we know his presence always, no matter where, no matter what."[8]

The most bone-chilling realization about our self-talk—that God hears every thought we think before we even think it—can also be our personal spiritual Great Awakening if we absorb the following three key principles into our lives.

1. Our spirit is hardwired into the Holy Spirit every moment of our lives.

Recently our church performed a drama where a man sat down

at breakfast to pray his usual "God-bless-my-day" prayer over his Pop-Tarts. When he opened his eyes, Jesus sat staring at him from across the table. It made for a hilarious sketch as Jesus silently walked beside the man through his day, beckoning and directing. Yet we were all poignantly reminded of the reality that Jesus is really with us as we munch on our Pop-Tarts or down our lattes. Yet we seldom act like we really believe Jesus is *really* there.

Through the Holy Spirit, I have constant access to God. Our battery connection can't go dead. Circuits can't overload. God won't put me on hold, and I don't have to worry about call-waiting.

My Father is a captive audience to my every thought, my every move. He listens for even the most subtle signs of my spirit stirring. He's with me even in my silences, and He longs for me to draw close and share my heartbreaks, pain, desires, and dreams.

2. Our self-talk can revolutionize our prayer life as we turn our self-talk into God-talk.

Once we've learned to turn up the volume and identify negative self-talk, life becomes an adventure in growing in Christ. Challenges become opportunities, and we lean into the expectancy of the *if—If* we truly believe God has our best interests at heart and we can fully trust Him, we strap ourselves to Him, face our fears, and leap in faith. Listening to our self-talk becomes a way of life.

So what does this look like in the day-to-day grind of life? Let's say Dan and I are tooling down the road. I'm frustrated because I want him to get gas before we leave town, but he wants to buy it farther into our trip because he thinks it will be cheaper. But when we get down the road and are forced to fill up, it's actually more expensive.

Suddenly a little voice pops up into my head and tells me to sigh, to roll my eyes, to fling out a sarcastic comment, to gently remind Dan that I was right and he was wrong. (After all, I *was* right, and he *was* wrong.)

But a voice stirs inside me, and I'm reminded that my behavior just *might* be self-serving. It might be intended to make Dan feel bad at my expense. The Holy Spirit prompts me to ask deeper questions—What's my motive? Why is it important for me to be right all the time, to feel superior, to make Dan feel bad? Am I really so bothered about fifty cents, or am I trying to feed my arrogance?

Suddenly, I recognize that the Spirit of God is with me in this. He's on my team, and He wants to use a stop at a gas station *for me.* In that fleeting moment of evaluation, I'm faced with a choice.

With a simple lift of my eyebrows or sigh and turn of my head, I can choose to speak the sin in my heart, or I can run to the Father in prayer.

What I say doesn't have to be profound. He's already listening. His Spirit stirred me to pause, to question, and to convict my heart. The words flow easily, and self-talk is transformed into prayer.

God, you know my stinky pride is kicking in again, but I'm fighting it. Please forgive me. I want to honor Dan right now. Give me grace to do something loving instead of something stupid and selfish. May the power of your Spirit rise up in me to choose obedience and to worship you in this very moment.

Prayer.

Repentance.

A change of attitude and direction.

And a speechless husband as I choose to run into the gas station and return with a Diet Coke and a kiss.

This is the power of our self-talk—the power to listen, to question, to repent, and to experience the power of a changed life as we turn to the Father in love.

3. Our self-talk is meant to be a source of grace, growth, and blessing in our lives so we can bless others.

The end of the double love command is a lifestyle of investment in others—the concern, sharing of troubles, and giving and receiving the apostle Paul mentions in Philippians 4:10–19. Our gifts become the wellspring for ministry in the lives of others, building the Body of Christ and bringing light to a dark world.

SELF-TALK AS TEACHER

A well-known self-image consultant and TV host recommends that people struggling with body image stand naked in front of a mirror and take a long and loving look at themselves. Most of us would probably find her suggestion daunting. Listening in on our self-talk can be a lot like standing naked in front of a mirror. If we're truthful with ourselves, we'll see a lot of things we'd really rather not look at.

But the naked truth about ourselves is that we come wired with the capacity for limitless change, with our own private tutor—a voice that shows us our dark side so we can find our way to the light. Twenty-four hours a day, seven days a week, our thoughts provide us with feedback on the state of our minds, wills, and emotions. And those same thoughts can provide us a path back to God.

God doesn't want our self-talk to make us self-aware. He wants it to change us—and not into good people, but into people who share the nature and mind of His Son, Jesus Christ. And so He placed His very Spirit in us to commune with our spirit, convict us, draw us, and teach us.

But beyond that, to conform us—to shape and mold our minds in order that we might be "a kind of firstfruits of all he created" (James 1:18). We're the crowning glory of God's creation, and the fruit of our lives is intended to bear harvests in future generations.

Stewardship of our self-talk has eternal consequences. It determines whether we bear fruit. It shapes the seeds of truth we sow in others and that they will sow in future generations. Every thought we take captive releases us to be more fruitful, as we follow our calling and set our hearts and minds on things above (Colossians 3:1–2).

Self-talk becomes a precious gift when we recognize that God is always present in our thoughts and that in the quickness of one breath, we can ask for a revived spirit, renewed heart, or insight into our souls.

Knowing how to use that gift can grow into a lifestyle of self-reflection, repentance, and obedience on the path to a righteous life.

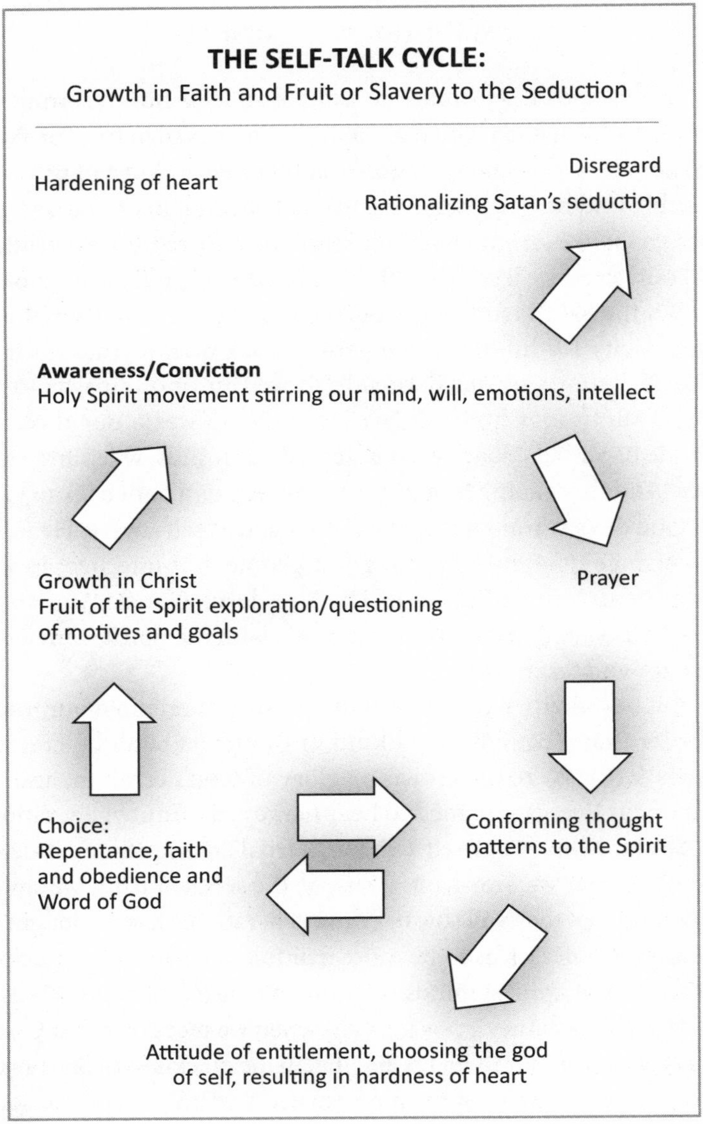

LISTEN UP: A WORD FROM JAMES

James, the half brother of Jesus and leader of the New Testament church at Jerusalem, gives us direction in regard to thinking and speaking:

> *Don't be deceived, my dear brothers. Every good and perfect gift is from above, coming down from the Father of the heavenly lights, who does not change like shifting shadows. He chose to give us birth through the word of truth, that we might be a kind of firstfruits of all he created.*
>
> *My dear brothers, take note of this: Everyone should be quick to listen, slow to speak and slow to become angry, for man's anger does not bring about the righteous life that God desires. Therefore, get rid of all moral filth and the evil that is so prevalent and humbly accept the word planted in you, which can save you. Do not merely listen to the word, and so deceive yourselves. Do what it says. Anyone who listens to the word but does not do what it says is like a man who looks at his face in a mirror and, after looking at himself, goes away and immediately forgets what he looks like. But the man who looks intently into the perfect law that gives freedom, and continues to do this, not forgetting what he has heard, but doing it—he will be blessed in what he does.*
>
> —James 1:16–25

James couldn't make our mission much more clear. We're the fruit of God's hands, blessed with His perfect gifts, selected as His chosen sons and daughters. Because of His great love, we're responsible for putting our roots down deep into the dirt of life and bringing forth fruit. We're to draw from His richness and burst forth with abundant life. But growth doesn't come automatically.

"Be quick to listen."

God's Spirit is at work in us, speaking, convicting, moving, stirring. But listening requires sifting through the dirt of our sin-tainted souls. Discernment takes work, and it's our job to pull out the weeds in our hearts.

"Be slow to speak and slow to become angry."

As we grow to love God more, we experience a Spirit-saturated desire to guard our tongues and actions because we're not controlled by simple self-will. Our thoughts become grafted to God's through moment-by-moment prayer that flows from gratitude that wells up from the deep knowledge that all we are, have, and ever will be we owe to our Father.

Our lives erupt in a doxology of praise as love spills from us and into the world—

life lived in expectancy,
in confidence,
in straining toward the righteous life that God desires.

"Therefore get rid of all moral filth and the evil that is so prevalent."

So we strain to listen to the Spirit of God, knowing that in listening we'll be changed and inch one step further into the life the Father envisioned for us in the garden.

But change is determined by the evil we're willing to lay aside, and letting go of evil is a decision that begins in the battleground of our minds.

We're called to a righteous life, and that life begins in our thoughts.

"And humbly accept the word planted in you which can save you."

God's Spirit and Word have been planted in the soil of our hearts as His gracious gifts of hope to us. We don't have to remain the struggling, proud, self-centered people we are. We can be changed!

As though we were master gardeners, we're called to tend the

Word planted in us and watch for the harvest of righteousness that is our calling in Jesus. We can listen to our hearts and nurture what God's planted within us, or we can allow the hardened, untended soil of our thought life to choke life from the seeds of truth.

It's been said that we lie loudest when we lie to ourselves.

"Do not merely listen to the word and deceive yourselves. Do what it says."

It's been said that we lie loudest when we lie to ourselves. Motives, actions, and good deeds that look shiny and succulent on the surface can be a bruised and mealy mess once we dig closer to the core.

Galatians 6:3–5 reminds us that we're easily deceived.

If anyone thinks he is something when he is nothing, he deceives himself. Each one should test his own actions. Then he can take pride in himself, without comparing himself to somebody else, for each one should carry his own load.

Carrying our load means, in part, honestly and transparently shouldering responsibility for the truth God's poured into us. It means sowing truth into the fiber of our being. The person who learns to do this can stand naked before God and look at herself honestly, joyfully, and with pride, knowing her Father is completing *His* work in and through her. Gratitude for God's gifts overflows in all she does—she's spotless in Christ, glorious in His perfection.

In contrast, James gives us an example of self-deception—a man so trapped by his self-perceptions that when he has an opportunity to look into a mirror and see what he truly looks like, he merely glances, then immediately forgets what he saw. Why? His mind was made up about who he was; he wasn't interested in how others perceived him, especially God.

James's point? Those who only glance at their souls, who aren't willing to look long and hard into a mirror and learn from what they see there, are self-deceived. Hebrews 13:15–16 goes on to encourage us in our fruit bearing.

> *Through Jesus, therefore, let us continually offer to God a sacrifice of praise—the fruit of lips that confess his name. And do not forget to do good and to share with others, for with such sacrifices God is pleased.*

"The man who looks intently into the perfect law that gives freedom, and continues to do this, not forgetting what he has heard, but doing it—he will be blessed in what he does."

In Genesis 3, the voice of the serpent whispered, and Eve forgot . . .

- her Creator's love for her
- her identity as a child of God
- her rich blessings.

Her thoughts plummeted into the abyss of entitlement, and she glanced away from true freedom. With a few fleeting thoughts, she forgot the voice of her Maker, stepped outside the boundaries of her true identity, and lost the blessings of her inheritance. But by the grace of God, Jesus Christ restored to us what once was lost. The curse of sin has been reversed, but not without consequences in this world. Our self-talk will always be a source of immeasurable growth and good. But it will also be the place where we, like Eve, will be most tempted to hide from God, from others, and even from ourselves.

Self-talk is our moment-by-moment opportunity for change and renewal. It is a gift for praise. For blessing. For creativity. For birthing and binding. It is power because it is rooted in our hearts, entwined with our spirits and the Holy Spirit in us. It is the aorta that connects us to our motives and is the means by which we look into God's perfect law that brings freedom.

Our self-talk can serve as a tree of life, bringing forth the fruit of righteousness, helping us remember what we've heard, prodding us to do what God's told us to do, and motivating us to bless and love others as we desire to be loved.

And this is my prayer:
that your love may abound more and more
in knowledge and in depth of insight,
so that you may be able to discern what is best
and may be pure and blameless until the day of Christ,
filled with the fruit of righteousness that comes through Jesus Christ—to the glory and praise of God.

—PHILIPPIANS 1:9–11

SOUL SEARCH
Breaking the Silence

- Look at the chart on page 156. Can you think of a time this week when you've felt the Spirit of God stirring your awareness of sin through your self-talk? What course did you follow on the chart? Can you follow your path of thought? Did you take steps toward growth and obedience in this experience? In what ways?
- In what ways do you struggle to be "quick to listen and slow to speak"? Do you feel the Spirit of God moving you to become a greater student of your self-talk? In what ways?

FACING THE SEDUCTION
Listening to the Spirit and the Word

- God has given us rich promises regarding our identity, our position, our power, our provision, and our protection. Flip to appendix 10, *Power in Your Self-Talk*. Choose three truths that are most meaningful to you from those listed and write them on 3 x 5 cards. Meditate and pray through them this week, asking God to reveal their truth to you in new and powerful ways.
- How can Philippians 1:9–11 be applied to your battle with your self-talk as you seek to harvest the fruit of righteousness?
    - in love
    - in knowledge
    - in wisdom
    - in discernment
- Galatians 6:4 tells us to "test [our] own actions." How does this passage relate to our self-talk?

RESPONDING FROM THE HEART
Prayer

Father God, this is my prayer, that my love would abound more and more toward You and toward others. That I would grow in knowledge and depth of insight, in discernment, and that I would be pure and blameless until the day of Christ, filled with the fruits of righteousness that come through Jesus Christ—to Your glory and Your praise.

Give me the heart of Jesus—to love as He loves. Give me discernment to see through my rationalizations and delusions so that I might love You with more passion each day. I lay all that I am and have at Your feet in humble submission, lifting my praise to You for Your promise to use me, fill me, and make me an instrument of blessing and grace to bring honor to You. Amen.

Notes

1. David J. Pollay, *What Did You Say?*, www.happynews.com/columns/david-j-pollay/592007/say.htm.
2. Matthew Henry, *Matthew Henry's Commentary Volume 1, Genesis to Joshua,* Genesis chapter 3 (Chicago: Fleming Revell, n.d.).
3. Mail Online News. *Jockey wins his first race after 28 years.* Last updated 24 November 2008, www.dailymail.co.uk/news/article-1088875/Jockey-wins-race-28-years-nearly-throws-away-early-victory-celebration.
4. BiBlos.com.scripturetext.com/proverbs/11-20.htm.
5. Kenneth S. Wuest, *Wuest's Word Studies from the Greek New Testament, Volume 3* (Grand Rapids: William B. Eerdmans, 1973), 81.
6. *Christian Examiner*, January/February 2004, as quoted in Rick Warren's Ministry Toolbox, www.pastors.com, Issue 150, http://legacy.pastors.com/RWMT/?ID=150.
7. BiBlos.com. *Jamieson-Fausset-Brown Bible Commentary.* Biblecommenter.com/Philippians/3-13/htm.
8. Abraham Kuyper, adapted by James C. Schaap, *Near Unto God* (Grand Rapids: Eerdmans, 1997), 23.

Appendix 1

Listening In on Your Self-Talk

Use the following assessment tool to informally assess your heart attitudes in your relationships with others, as well as your internal dialogues. You may choose to focus on one question at a time, meditating on that question for a day or perhaps a week as you evaluate the manner in which you speak to yourself. Pray through each of these areas, asking the Holy Spirit to apply His truth to your heart as you seek answers.

PROTECTING OURSELVES

I often find myself carrying on defensive conversations and justifying my actions to others, both internally and externally.	I am willing and able to admit my weaknesses and flaws and humbly accept constructive criticism from others.

1 2 3 4 5 6 7 8 9 10

It's difficult for me to admit failure; I struggle to allow people to see an unflawed version of who I am.	I'm able to admit failure and allow people to see my flaws.

1 2 3 4 5 6 7 8 9 10

I dislike having people approach me with criticism and typically respond with defensiveness.	I have a spirit that's open and approachable and responds to criticism or correction with a humble, listening heart.

1 2 3 4 5 6 7 8 9 10

I feel a compulsion to prove myself right when people believe wrong of me.	I am able to let things go and allow God to be my defender.

1 2 3 4 5 6 7 8 9 10

I mistrust God, His inherent goodness, and His plans for me.	I rest in the character of God, despite the circumstances of my life.

1 2 3 4 5 6 7 8 9 10

I dislike exploring who other people are and tend to focus conversations on myself and my interests.	I actively explore who other people are and ask questions that show curiosity about their interests.

1 2 3 4 5 6 7 8 9 10

I constantly focus on what others think of me.	I'm able to rest in the confidence that I'm God's precious child and His image bearer, of eternal and inestimable value.

1 2 3 4 5 6 7 8 9 10

POSITIONING OURSELVES

When people are speaking, I'm usually formulating my responses in my head.	When people are speaking, I'm usually listening empathetically and actively.

1 2 3 4 5 6 7 8 9 10

I often find ways to blame others.	I'm quick to take responsibility for my own actions.

1 2 3 4 5 6 7 8 9 10

I trivialize others in my thinking and do not give them their proper place as image bearers of God, often disrespecting the talents God's given them and the roles they were created to fulfill.	I am quick to give others honor and respect, despite their station in life, respecting the talents God's given them and the roles they were created to fulfill.

1 2 3 4 5 6 7 8 9 10

I often find myself "measuring people up" as I'm interacting with them—judging their clothing, makeup, attitudes, conversation, opinions to find my advantage.	I'm able to approach and interact with people with a genuine interest in who they are and a heart that yearns to genuinely know them.

PROMOTING OURSELVES

I offer my opinions frequently, even when I'm not asked for them.	I'm quick to listen, slow to judge, and slow to speak.

1 2 3 4 5 6 7 8 9 10

I often find myself judging the flaws and sins of others, evaluating them against my personal standards.	I have a broken and contrite spirit and am aware of my imperfections and God's grace, which is reflected in a spirit of compassion and grace in judging others.

1 2 3 4 5 6 7 8 9 10

When I'm in a new environment, I find myself constantly assessing things around me against my personal standards.	When I'm in a new environment, I'm open and curious about those around me, seeking ways to learn to minister.

1 2 3 4 5 6 7 8 9 10

PROCURING POWER

I often find myself looking for ways to manipulate people to be used for my means or to promote my agenda.	I am aware of my desires for control and relinquish them to God; I honor people as God's image bearers and seek their best interests first, in accordance with the double love command.

1 2 3 4 5 6 7 8 9 10

I find myself compelled to make those around me think and behave like me.	I recognize that I was not created to be in control of the choices of others.

1 2 3 4 5 6 7 8 9 10

In situations of dissension and conflict, I gravitate toward those who share my opinion, often seeking to gauge other peoples' positions so I can hear my own position affirmed.	In situations of dissension and conflict, I strive to retain an open spirit and seek peace; I am quick to listen and slow to speak.

1 2 3 4 5 6 7 8 9 10

I have a haughty and demanding spirit that manifests itself in my desire to have my own way, seek my own good, and have others serve my own best interests.	I have a servant's heart that manifests itself in my desire to love God with all my heart, soul, and mind, and to love my neighbor as myself.

1 2 3 4 5 6 7 8 9 10

I like to exert control over other people, situations, and life in general.	I am able to allow others to be in control and to trust God for outcomes.

1 2 3 4 5 6 7 8 9 10

I hold grudges against others, replaying conversations and scenarios over and over in my head.	I am quick to forgive as an overwhelming response to God's outpouring of forgiveness and grace in my life and relinquish my hold on offenses through the power of the Holy Spirit.

1 2 3 4 5 6 7 8 9 10

PLUNDERING

I often see people and circumstances in light of the way I can use them to my advantage.	I see people and circumstances as opportunities to lovingly minister for the kingdom of God.

1 2 3 4 5 6 7 8 9 10

I have a heart for taking, even when it might cost someone else something.	I have a heart for giving, even when it costs me something.

1 2 3 4 5 6 7 8 9 10

When I enter a room, I typically size people up.	When I enter a room, I look for opportunities to serve.

1 2 3 4 5 6 7 8 9 10

I don't like to tithe, give to the poor, or to other needs where I don't have a vested interest or control.	I tithe and give generously out of gratitude to God, without strings.

1 2 3 4 5 6 7 8 9 10

LOVING BETTER

Choose three of the questions above and list a few simple strategies for (1) conforming your self-talk to a biblical model of Christ's love in those areas and, (2) taking positive steps toward changing your behavior.

Conforming Self-Talk in Love

1.

2.

3.

Taking Steps to Change Behavior

1.

2.

3.

Appendix 2

Tuning In to Motives and Goals

Our self-talk shapes our perceptions of truth, but we're often unaware of our inner dialogues. For instance, we may have wronged a friend and we feel a crushing weight of guilt and carry an almost palpable sense of remorse for having done something we know we shouldn't have done.

On the other hand, we may have wronged a friend and felt justified about our actions, so we find ourselves rationalizing our actions to a third party. Through our self-talk, we convince ourselves that our actions were defensible, perhaps even honorable. But as we carry on our self-talk, we may be oblivious to the values we apply to our internal debate.

Unawareness of our inner dialogues over a given situation					Awareness of our inner dialogues over a given situation				
1	2	3	4	5	6	7	8	9	10

For the believer, it's important to elevate subtle self-talk to conscious awareness in order to avoid the trap of self-deception:

- What am I actually telling myself through my self-talk? What "positions" am I formulating?
- Is what I'm telling myself consistent with biblical truth? In what ways?

- Does my decision reflect stewardship of my time, talent, and treasure?
- What are my motives? Are they pure, or do I have deeper hidden motives? How are my motives influencing my desires, expectations, agendas, behaviors?
- Am I committed to striving to live out the double love command in all areas of my life?
- How does my decision reflect my love for God?
- How does my decision reflect my love for others as I love myself?
- How does my decision reflect the love of God to a watching world?

Appendix 3

Learning to Listen to the Voice of the Spirit

How do I know if the voices stirring in my heart are the voices of the Spirit of God within me? Galatians 5:22 spells out the fruit of the Spirit in the believer's life. Use the following simple tool to help evaluate yourself in each of the following areas:

motives	behaviors
thoughts	desires
words	expectations
actions	agendas

Does not advance the double love command	Advances the double love command

in the following areas:

expressing love, joy, peace, patience, kindness, goodness, faithfulness, gentleness, self-control

1 2 3 4 5 6 7 8 9 10

In the area of my life in question, each of the areas above is:

In conflict with the Word of God	Consistent with the Word of God

1 2 3 4 5 6 7 8 9 10

In the area of my life in question, my actions and attitudes are:

In conflict with the counsel of godly church leaders and accountability partners	Affirmed by the counsel of leaders and accountability partners

1 2 3 4 5 6 7 8 9 10

I am unwilling to submit to what I believe to be biblically true and expected of me.					I am willing to submit to what I believe to be biblically true and expected of me.				
1	2	3	4	5	6	7	8	9	10

Appendix 4

The Seven Habits of Highly Effective Listeners

1. Learn to be a student of your own heart as you observe yourself.
2. Think in terms of life change.
3. Prepare for a marathon as you reshape lifelong patterns of thinking.
4. Commit to the disciplines of self-examination, reflection, and prayer.
5. Find an accountability partner.
6. Rely upon Scripture and the power of the Holy Spirit to convict, speak, and transform.
7. Learn the power of positive praise.

Appendix 5

Exploring Your Self-Talk

The lies that Satan birthed in Eve's heart are the whisperings that have resonated in the hearts of mankind from that moment in the garden and throughout history. Sometimes we are fully aware of these thoughts as they play through our minds, and sometimes we just don't listen to the way we talk to ourselves. But through repeated sin, the infiltration of culture, and our propensity to become calloused to the way which sin has twisted our thought processes, we often lose the battle for truth without even knowing our minds and hearts have become a war zone.

Satan's lies fall into five basic categories: **Gagging God** (doubting His character and pure intentions for our lives), **Opposing God** (challenging God's truth), **Outwitting God** (devising our own plans for our lives and refusing to submit to God), **Equaling God** (believing in our power to control and shape our eternal destiny apart from God), **Yielding to My Desires** (living a life based on pursuing whatever pleasures, goals, or desires we believe will bring self-fulfillment, apart from obedience to God).

The questions in each of the following categories are intended to help you explore your self-talk. God's Word clearly relates to each of the issues raised in the questions. It is recommended that you spend time in prayer prior to this exercise and consider these questions in small increments (perhaps even one at a time), asking the Holy Spirit to reveal the sin of your own heart so that you can experience brokenness and healing and begin to take steps toward restoration.

GAGGING GOD

1. I sometimes believe that God is responsible for messing up my life or the lives of those I love. If He's not responsible for messing things up, He at least doesn't care enough to intervene.
2. I believe that God is out there somewhere in heaven, watching my life from a distance, restricting me, and judging the things I do.
3. I'm not certain that God really exists at all, or if He does, that He's the God of the Bible or that I can be certain about that.
4. Now and then I allow myself a little gossip, a little slander, or a self-indulgent attitude. I hold the occasional grudge, or I even the playing field a bit when someone stomps on me or my loved ones. I think people are occasionally entitled to those kinds of attitudes.
5. When I think about God, my thoughts are generally great thoughts about His sovereignty, goodness, holiness, mercy, and His great love for me. Or on the contrary, when I think about God, I think of His judgment, disfavor, unfairness, and His toleration of me.

OPPOSING GOD

1. I'm not certain the Bible is really true, or that all of it is true, or why it should be some kind of standard for my life.
2. I believe I'm free to pick and choose the things in the Bible that best apply to my circumstances.
3. Sometimes it makes the best sense to apply truth for my life from the sources that best seem to fit what I need—world religions, philosophies, popular psychology, or whatever I've found that seems to work.
4. I believe that the most important things in my life are happiness and self-fulfillment.

5. It's okay with me to do and say things sometimes that contradict what's in the Bible.

OUTWITTING GOD

1. Even though the Bible speaks against some things and calls them sin, I believe I'm responsible for making the choices and plans that are best for me.
2. I sometimes/often feel the Holy Spirit tugging at my heart, but I go ahead and do what I want to do anyway.
3. I struggle with wanting to come up with my own plans apart from God or in opposition to God in the following areas:
    - My finances
    - My marriage
    - My job
    - My future
    - My past—forgiveness, reconciliation, restitutio
    - Stewardship of what God has given me—time, talent, money, resources, relationships
    - My level of respect in dealing with people and regarding them as image bearers
    - Control of my body—weight, addictions, stewardship of physical and emotional health
    - Control of my emotions
    - Control of my tongue
    - A lifestyle of commitment to faith and repentance

EQUALING GOD

1. I believe I'm in charge of deciding what's right and wrong for my life.
2. In certain areas where the Bible seems to teach one thing, I've chosen to go my own way and do something else.

3. Culture, other systems of faith, and popular teaching say that I can control my destiny through the power of positive thinking. I believe this might be true.
4. When I know biblical truth and I choose to do something else, I'm making myself my own god. I /often/seldom/frequently do this.
5. I believe that what we have the power to believe, we have the power to achieve because Jesus has promised us the power of His Holy Spirit.

YIELDING TO MY DESIRES

1. When I see something that I believe will fulfill my desires, I go after it.
2. When I'm faced with a desire for something that I want but that I question may be "right" for me, I ask myself whether or not pursuing this thing will satisfy me in order to find my answer.
3. What I "desire" is based on what looks and feels good, and brings the outcome I want.
4. In the past, I've yielded to desires that I knew were wrong in order to get what I wanted.
5. I believe that desires in and of themselves are not bad but the motives and goals behind those desires may be good or bad. I can think of examples when I have displayed both good and bad motives and goals in fulfilling my desires.

Appendix 6

Learning to Live in the If *of Expectancy*

We can actively **choose** to change our attitudes and our minds about the way we think (Philippians 2:5). We can learn to think like Christ, and Philippians chapter 2 shows us key principles to creating a mind-set for living a life in the ***if of expectancy***. Our thinking will be transformed as we understand the magnitude of what God did for us through Jesus Christ. We're empowered through the Holy Spirit to grow in wisdom and gain God's perspective on our relationships with others, on our view of and relationship with God, attitudes toward ourselves, and our purpose for our lives.

Philippians 2:1—"If you have any **encouragement from being united** with Christ."
How can being united with Christ encourage us and change our self-talk when:

- we're discouraged
- we're frustrated at our circumstances
- we're frustrated with other people and want to retaliate
- we want to lash out in anger
- we want to demand our own way
- we want to control and manipulate

How can being united with Christ change my self-talk in regard to my tendency to:

- protect myself, no matter what
- position myself to achieve the greatest possible advantage over others
- promote myself and my agendas
- procure power to accomplish my goals

- plunder from others and take what belongs to them for myself (their attention, their success, their respect, their belongings, their reputation)

How can being united with Christ change my self-talk in the following areas, especially considering Philippians 2:

- being like-minded with Christian brothers and sisters, having the same spirit and purpose (2:2)
- doing nothing out of selfish ambition or vain conceit (2:3)
- in humility considering others better than myself (2:3)
- looking not only to my interests but to the interests of others (2:4)
- having the attitude of Jesus Christ (2:5–8)
- not grasping in my attitude (2:6)
- not fighting with God's character or agenda
- making my agenda second to God's
- choosing the nature of a servant (2:7)
- humbling myself (2:8)
- becoming obedient (2:8)
- knowing I'm called to "work out (figure out how to live out) my salvation with fear and trembling" (2:12)
- knowing God works in me according to His purposes (2:13)
- doing everything without complaining or arguing (2:14)
- knowing my blameless and pure conduct as a child of God should shine like stars in a crooked and depraved world (2:15)
- knowing my task is to hold out the word of life—to bring joy to the name of Jesus Christ (2:16–18)

Appendix 7
Scripture References to Common Needs

Abiding: Psalm 119:15–16, Psalm 119:105, John 15:1–4, John 15:7, Colossians 3:15–17, James 4:8, 1 John 2:24–25, 1 John 3:6

Access to God: 2 Samuel 22:7, Psalm 4:3, Psalm 28:6–7, Psalm 34:4–7, Psalm 120:1, John 14:13–14, Hebrews 4:16, James 5:16, 1 Peter 3:12, Matthew 7:7–8

Adoration: 1 Chronicles 16:29, Psalm 46:10–11, Psalm 48:1, Psalm 95:6, Psalm 100:4–5, Psalm 108:1–5, Psalm 117:1–2, Romans 14:11, 2 Corinthians 1:3

Anger: Psalm 30:5, Psalm 145:8, Proverbs 14:7, Proverbs 15:8, Proverbs 16:23, Proverbs 19:11, Proverbs 22:24–25, Ecclesiastes 4:31–32, Colossians 3:21

Answered Prayer: Psalm 91:15–16, Jeremiah 33:3, Matthew 7:7–8, Matthew 7:11, Matthew 18:19–20, John 14:13–14, Ephesians 3:20–21, 1 Thessalonians 5:16–18, 1 Thessalonians 5:24, Hebrews 4:16, Hebrews 11:6, James 1:5–6, James 5:16, 1 John 3:22

Attitudes: Proverbs 4:23, Micah 6:8, Galatians 5:16, Galatians 5:22–23, Ephesians 4:31–32, Ephesians 5:1–2, Philippians 2:5–8, Philippians 2:14

Blessing: Psalm 1:1–3, Psalm 112:1–3, Matthew 7:7–8, 1 Corinthians 2:9–10, Ephesians 1:3, Ephesians 3:20–21, Philippians 4:19

Brokenness: Psalm 34:18–19, Psalm 51:1, 6, 9, 10, 12–13, 17, John 15:5, Philippians 4:13, James 4:6–7, 10

Comfort: Psalm 18:2, Psalm 37:39, Psalm 46:1–3, Psalm 55:22, Psalm 119:50, Isaiah 49:13, Matthew 11:28, John 14:16,

John 14:26, John 16:33, 2 Corinthians 1:3–4, 2 Thessalonians 2:16–17

Commitment and Endurance: Psalm 37:3–7, Matthew 10:32, Matthew 10:38–39, 2 Timothy 1:12, Hebrews 10:35–36, Hebrews 11:6, Hebrews 12:1–2, James 4:7–8, James 5:11

Compassion: Psalm 86:15, Micah 6:8, Zechariah 7:9–10, Matthew 9:36, Galatians 6:1–2, Hebrews 4:14–15, 1 Peter 3:8

Contentment: Proverbs 3:6, Isaiah 26:3–4, John 14:27, Romans 8:28, Philippians 4:6–7, Philippians 4:11, Philippians 4:13, 1 Timothy 6:6–8, Hebrews 13:5

Courage: Deuteronomy 3:5–6, Psalm 27:14, Psalm 31:24, Isaiah 40:29, Isaiah 41:10, Isaiah 43:1, Isaiah 54:17, Romans 6:37–39, Hebrews 10:22–23, I John 4:18

Death: Psalm 23:4, Psalm 48:14, Psalm 49:15, Psalm 73:26, Proverbs 14:32, Isaiah 25:8, Romans 8:38–39, 1 Corinthians 15:55, 2 Corinthians 4:16, Hebrews 2:14–15

Deliverance, Protection, and Help: 2 Samuel 22:2–4, Psalm 34:4–6, Psalm 46:1–2, Psalm 50:14–15, Jeremiah 29:12–14, Joel 2:32, Romans 8:37, Philippians 4:13, 19, 1 John 3:22, Jude 24–25

Discernment: John 15:14–15, Romans 8:6, 1 Corinthians 2:14–15

Discipleship: Psalm 119:105, Luke 9:23–24, John 13:34–35, John 15:8, John 15:10–12, Colossians 3:16–17, 2 Timothy 2:15

Discipline: 1 Kings 8:61, Psalm 25:4, John 14:15, 1 Corinthians 10:4–5, Hebrews 12:6–8, James 1:22

Enemies: Deuteronomy 20:4, Psalm 27:5–6, Psalm 37:40, Psalm 60:12, Proverbs 16:7, Isaiah 54:17

Eternal Life: John 6:47, John 11:25–26, 1 Corinthians 15:51–54, John 3:16, 1 Thessalonians 4:16–17, 1 John 5:13, 1 John 2:25, Revelation 7:15–17

Evangelism: Luke 15:4–7, Acts 1:8, 2 Timothy 2:15, 1 Peter 3:15, 2 Peter 3:9

Faith: Matthew 11:22–24, Matthew 17:20, Luke 1:37, John 15:7, Romans 10:17, Ephesians 3:20, Ephesians 6:16, Philippians 4:19, Colossians 2:6–7, Hebrews 11:1, 6, 1 John 5:4

Fear: Psalm 46:1, Proverbs 1:33, Proverbs 3:24–26, Isaiah 41:14, Matthew 10:28, Mark 4:40, Luke 12:32, John 14:27, Romans 8:15, 2 Timothy 1:7

Forgiveness: Matthew 5:44–45, Matthew 6:12, Matthew 6:14–15, Mark 11:25–26, Luke 6:35–37, Luke 7:47, John 3:16, Romans 12:20, Ephesians 1:6–7, 1 John 1:9, 1 John 4:19–21

Future: Psalm 23:4, Psalm 23:6, Proverbs 3:5–6, Matthew 6:34, John 11:25, John 14:1–3, 1 John 5:11

Giving: Psalm 41:1–2, Proverbs 11:24–25, Matthew 6:1–4, Matthew 6:19–21, Luke 6:38, 2 Corinthians 9:7, 1 Timothy 6:17–18

Gossip: Leviticus 19:16, Psalm 34:13, Psalm 52:2, Proverbs 11:9, Proverbs 16:28, Proverbs 18:8, Proverbs 20:19, Proverbs 25:23, Proverbs 26:20–22

Growth: Psalm 92:12, Ephesians 3:16–17, Ephesians 4:14–15, Philippians 1:6, Philippians 1:9–10, Colossians 3:16, 1 Peter 2:2–3

Guidance: Joshua 1:8, Psalm 73:23–24, Psalm 119:11, Psalm 119:105, Proverbs 6:22–23, Proverbs 16:9, Isaiah 30:21, Romans 8:14, 2 Peter 1:4

Guilt: Psalm 103:11–13, Isaiah 43:25, Isaiah 55:7, Jeremiah 31:34, 2 Corinthians 5:17, 1 John 1:7, 9, 1 John 2:12, 1 John 3:19–20

Healing: Psalm 30:2, Psalm 103:3, Psalm 107:20, Psalm 147:3, Matthew 9:35, James 5:14–15, 3 John 2

Heaven: Matthew 5:10, 12, John 14:1–3, John 14:6, 1 Corinthians 2:9, 1 Corinthians 13:12, 2 Peter 3:13, Revelation 21:4

Help in Trouble: Job 5:19, Job 8:20–21, Psalm 9:9, Psalm 22:24, Psalm 31:23, Psalm 32:7, Psalm 37:39, Psalm 71:20, Psalm 91:10–11, Psalm 146:8

Honesty: Leviticus 19:11, Deuteronomy 25:15–16, Proverbs 11:1, Proverbs 16:8, Proverbs 20:10, 23, Micah 6:10–12, Colossians 3:9–10, 1 Thessalonians 4:6–7

Hope: Psalm 42:11, Psalm 71:5, 14, Jeremiah 17:7, Zechariah 9:12, Romans 4:18, Romans 5:5, Romans 15:13, Hebrews 6:18–19, 1 Peter 1:13

Humility: Psalm 10:17, Proverbs 16:19, Matthew 18:4, Matthew 23:12, Luke 14:11, Philippians 2:3, James 4:6, James 4:10, 1 Peter 5:5–7

Identity: Psalm 139, Zephaniah 3:17, John 1:9–12a, Romans 5:7–8, Romans 8:16–17a, 1 Corinthians 2:9b, Galatians 3:26, Galatians 4:6–7, Ephesans 1:11–12, 1 Thessalonians 5:24, James 1:18, 1 John 3:1a

Jealousy: Deuteronomy 5:21, Psalm 10:3, Psalm 37:7, Proverbs 3:31, Proverbs 14:30, Proverbs 27:4, 1 Corinthians 10:24, Galatians 5:26, James 3:14, 16, James 4:5

Joy and Happiness: Nehemiah 8:10, Psalm 16:11, Psalm 45:7–8, Psalm118:24, Proverbs 15:13, John 15:11–12, Romans 8:28

Kindness: Nehemiah 9:17, Romans 12:9–21, Galatians 5:22–23

Life: Psalm 90:12–13, John 3:16, John 10:10, Romans 6:23, Galatians 2:20, 1 John 5:12, Revelation 2:10

Loneliness: Genesis 28:15, Psalm 40:17, Isaiah 43:4, Isaiah 58:9, John 14:16, 2 Corinthians 6:18, Colossians 2:10

Love: John 3:16–17, Romans 5:8, Romans 8:38–39, Romans 13:10, 1 Corinthians 12:31, 1 Corinthians 13:1–13, Galatians 5:14, 1 John 4:7–8, 1 John 4:18

Lust: Proverbs 6:25–29, Matthew 5:27–28, 2 Timothy 2:22, James 4:1–4, James 4:7–8, 1 Peter 1:14–16, 1 Peter 2:11, 1 John 2:16–17

Lying: Leviticus 19:12, Deuteronomy 19:16–19, Proverbs 14:5, Proverbs 19:5, 9, Proverbs 24:28, Proverbs 25:18, Revelation 21:8

Meekness: Psalm 22:26, Psalm 25:9, Psalm 37:11, Proverbs 15:1, Isaiah 11:4, Isaiah 29:19, Zephaniah 2:3, Matthew 5:5, 1 Peter 3:4

Mercy: 1 Chronicles 16:34, Psalm 36:7–10, Psalm 51:1, Psalm 103:17, Micah 6:8

Money: Job 5:15–16, Psalm 9:18, Psalm 12:5, Proverbs 11:28, Proverbs 23:4–5, Proverbs 28:20, Ecclesiastes 4:6, Ecclesiastes 5:12–14

Obedience: Deuteronomy 11:26–28, Deuteronomy 13:4, Isaiah 1:19, Micah 6:8, John 14:15, John 14:21, John 14:23, Romans 12:1–2, Hebrews 5:8–9

Patience: Psalm 37:7–9, Psalm 40:1–3, Psalm 62:5–6, Romans 15:5, Hebrews 6:12, Hebrews 10:36–37, 2 Peter 1:6

Peace: Psalm 29:11, Psalm 119:165, Isaiah 26:3, John 14:27, Romans 5:1, Romans 8:28, Galatians 5:22, Philippians 4:6–7

Power and Might: Psalm 119:11, Matthew 28:18, Acts 1:8, Romans 8:37, 2 Corinthians 12:9, Galatians 2:20, Ephesians 3:16, 20, Ephesians 6:10–11, Philippians 2:9, Philippians 4:13, Colossians 1:11–12, Hebrews 4:12, 2 Peter 1:4, Revelation 4:11

Prayer: Psalm 34:17, Psalm 65:2, Psalm 55:17, Psalm 145:18–19, Proverbs 15:29, Isaiah 30:19, Isaiah 65:24, Matthew 6:6–8, Matthew 7:1, John 14:13–14, John 15:7, James 5:16, 1 John 3:22

Presence of God: Exodus 33:14, Psalm 16:11, Psalm 46:1, Matthew 28:20, Hebrews 13:5–6

Pride: Psalm 119:21, Proverbs 8:13, Proverbs 16:18, Proverbs 21:4, Proverbs 26:12, Proverbs 28:25–26, Mark 9:35, Luke

16:15, John 5:44, 2 Corinthians 10:17–18

Prosperity: Psalm 1:3, Psalm 92:14, Jeremiah 31:12, John 15:1–5, 2 Peter 1:8

Protection: Job 11:18–19, Psalm 4:8, Psalm 27:1, Psalm 91:9–10, Psalm 112:7, Proverbs 3:24, Proverbs 18:10, 1 Peter 3:13

Repentance: John 3:16, Acts 3:19, Romans 2:4, 2 Corinthians 7:9–10, Timothy 2:24–26, 2 Peter 3:9, 1 John 1:9

Righteousness: Psalm 5:8, Psalm 23:3, Psalm 84:11, Proverbs 12:2, Isaiah 3:10, Matthew 6:33, 1 Corinthians 1:30

Salvation: John 1:12–13, John 3:3–7, Romans 5:15, 2 Corinthians 5:17, 2 Corinthians 5:21, Ephesians 2:5, Colossians 2:13, 1 Timothy 2:3–4, 1 Timothy 4:9–10, Titus 3:4–6, 1 John 2:1–2

Self-Control: Matthew 5:39–41, Matthew 16:24–26, Luke 18:29–30, Romans 8:12–13, Galatians 5:22–24, Titus 2:11–12, 1 Peter 1:13, 2 Peter 1:4–8

Sexual Sin: 1 Corinthians 1:8–9, 1 Corinthians 6:13–15, 1 Corinthians 6:18–20, 1 Corinthians 7:1, 1 Corinthians 7:37, 1 Corinthians 10:13, 1 Thessalonians 4:3, Hebrews 13:4, James 1:13–15, 2 Peter 2:9

Shame: Psalm 119:1–6, Romans 5:1–5, Romans 10:11, 2 Timothy 1:12, 2 Timothy 2:15, 1 Peter 4:16

Sound Mind: Isaiah 41:10, 2 Corinthians 1:3–4, Philippians 4:6–8, 2 Timothy 1:7

Strength: Psalm 27:1, Psalm 28:7, Psalm 84:5, 2 Corinthians 12:9, Ephesians 3:16–17, Philippians 4:13

Success, Prosperity, and Provision: Joshua 1:7–8, Psalm 91:15–16, Ecclesiastes 10:10, Matthew 6:33, Matthew 7:7–8, 11, Philippians 4:19

Temptation: Psalm 119:11, Matthew 4:4–11, Matthew 26:41, Luke 22:40, 1 Corinthians 10:12–13

Thanksgiving: Deuteronomy 3:24, Psalm 92:1, Psalm 100:3–4, Psalm 103:1–5, Psalm 139:14, 1 Thessalonians 5:16–18

Trust: Psalm 23:4, Psalm 112:7, Proverbs 3:5–6, 1 Corinthians 10:13, 2 Corinthians 3:4–6, 1 Timothy 6:17–18

Truth: Psalm 51:5–10, Psalm 91:4, Proverbs 23:23, John 8:32, John 14:6, Ephesians 4:15, 25

Understanding: Job 32:8, Psalm 90:12, Psalm 111:10, Psalm 119:27, Psalm 119:33–34, Psalm 119:105, Proverbs 4:5–7

Victory: 1 Corinthians 15:54–58, 1 John 5:4–5

Wisdom: Proverbs 8:14, Proverbs 16:22, 1 Corinthians 2:14–15, James 1:5

Word of God: Deuteronomy 11:18, Joshua 1:8, Psalm 119:105, Psalm 119:130, Proverbs 6:23, John 5:39, Romans 1:16, Romans 10:17, Hebrews 4:12, 1 Peter 1:12, 1 Peter 1:25, 1 Peter 2:2, 2 Timothy 3:15–16, Revelation 1:3

Worry: Psalm 9:9–10, Psalm 32:7, Psalm 46:1–3, Psalm 91:15, Isaiah 32:17, Jeremiah 17:8, Luke 10:41–42, Romans 8:28, 2 Corinthians 4:8–9, Philippians 4:6–7, Philippians 4:19

Appendix 8
Listening to Your Self-Talk through Journaling

Part 1

For the next two weeks, keep a notebook close at hand and focus on the inner dialogues playing out in your mind, especially when you're in stressful or anxiety-producing situations. Listen to the things you're telling yourself as you jot down notes; identify your self-talk as either true or a lie according to biblical principles.

- Myself—Have I remembered I'm a child of God?
- Others—Have I seen others as being made in God's image?
- Relationships
- Responsibilities
- Circumstances, past and present
- Other

Example:

This morning when I accidentally drove through the ditch when I pulled out of the driveway I told myself I never do anything right. It's just another example of the loser I am.

This is a lie. I'm always putting myself down.

Then see appendix 7 under the category of "Guilt" for Scripture to help conform your self-talk to the Word of God. Choose one verse or perhaps one phrase from one verse to meditate on to help transform your thinking. Example from Psalm 103:11–13: I am not a loser, I'm eternally valuable and adored by the God of the universe. This should be "identity in Christ" instead of guilt. Guilt implies sin, not merely making a mistake. Do you want to add identity as a category to appendix 7?

Part 2

As you begin to identify the lies you commonly tell yourself, spend time in prayer, asking the Spirit of God to reveal your deeper motives. Are you angry at God? If so, why? Have you been harboring a desire for revenge toward someone? An attitude of bitterness or unforgiveness? What about a haughty and prideful spirit that tells you that the world/your workplace/your family would be better off if you could be in charge?

To get at our motives, it's often helpful to ask ourselves *why* we believe something to be true and *what we're trying to accomplish* through our actions, words, or attitudes. Our first response will often be a superficial response as we ask ourselves these questions because more than one truth can be operational in our lives at one time—"I'm yelling because I'm trying to get my kids to listen to me for once." But a second or third pass through the question will often get us to our deeper motives if we're honest with ourselves—"I'm yelling because I'm venting my rage," or "I'm yelling because I'm ashamed of the way my kids are acting in public right now because it makes me look like a bad parent."

The first requirement for a changed heart is a broken and contrite one. God passionately desires to conform us to the image of His Son, and that can only be done if we're first willing to humbly confess that we're broken deep inside and need to be changed.

If, for instance, you discover that you've been justifying the sin of raging in anger at your children, (1) confess that sin to God, (2) accept His free and full forgiveness, (3) begin to transform your thinking with truth from Scripture that applies to your situation and your power in Christ, (4) tell someone and enlist an accountability partner in helping you reclaim this area of your life.

Appendix 9

Listening to Your Self-Talk in the Clamor of Life

Thinking about stewardship in terms of time, talent, and treasure is a familiar concept. But we'll never be good stewards of anything if we're not first good stewards of our thought life. Yet, how often do we scrutinize our thinking to see if what we believe is truth or lies?

Our self-talk is shaped by hundreds of factors, but a good starting point in evaluating our view of the world is to look at the most influential factors that shape our lives and ask a few basic questions.

FAMILY IMPACT ON MY SELF-TALK
CONSIDER THE FOLLOWING:

1. Did/does my family convey attitudes of respect, dignity, honor, and esteem for others, even the unlovely, disenfranchised, or those different from us?
2. Did/does my family convey unconditional love, respect, dignity, honor, and esteem for me and other family members?
3. Did/does my family love and serve God?
4. Did/does my parent/s model and teach a balanced work ethic and godly stewardship of time, talents, and treasures?
5. Did/does my family accept the Bible and biblical values as authoritative and practical for everyday living?

6. What impact did/does each of these have on my thinking and self-talk?

Friends Repeat the above exercise, but substitute "friends" for "family."

CULTURE AND HERITAGE

In what ways did/does my culture or my heritage influence my thinking and self-talk in the following areas:

a. Family dynamics, structure, roles, and communication
b. Communication with others
c. Worship styles and beliefs
d. View of time/timeliness/relationship of value to time
e. Regard for the aged/elderly
f. Attitudes toward childrearing
g. Views toward money, spending, giving, tithing, stewardship
h. Attitudes toward those who are different

As you consider the term *culture,* also think about the impact of church cultures, community cultures, educational cultures—how have these influenced your self-talk in positive and negative ways?

WOUNDS

Read the following questions and answer: How did/does this affect my thinking and self-talk?

- Am I aware of the wounds of my past, and have I done the work of forgiving those who have wronged me?

- Do I believe that God is working out His perfect plan for me and that He weaves all things together for my good and equips me with every resource I need to live abundantly, in spite of painful circumstances?
- Do I believe that God gives me the power to forgive anyone, under any circumstances, and to bring glory to Him through my life, in spite of my past?
- Am I willing to forget what is behind and strive toward my calling to become like Jesus—to conform my mind to His through faith?
- Do I believe I am forgivable?

Appendix 10

Power in Your Self-Talk—Blessings and Affirmations from the Word of God

Adapted with permission from
Blessing Your Spirit with the Blessings of Your Father and the Names of God
by Sylvia Gunter and Arthur Burk
The Father's Business: www.thefathersbusiness.com

MY IDENTITY

I am a special creation of God, uniquely designed and crafted in love in the details of my body and personality.

God formed a plan with eternal purpose for me before the world was spun on its axis.

My life is intentional, and I was crafted by God. He superintends even the imperfect parts to work out His sovereign plan.

Because of God's sovereignty, I can live purposefully and victoriously above even the painful and difficult aspects of my family background.

God delights in my nurture and well-being.

I am blessed with a heart identity as God's own child, securely loved.

I am blessed with the guiding and equipping of the Holy Spirit, who develops and completes my identity.

I can know peace, based on my identity as a child of God and my Father's provision, protection, and purposes for me.

Because I am blessed with my Father's power, I am strengthened, sustained, and renewed in my spirit to be who I am called to be.

MY PURPOSE

I exist because I am part of God's plan. I have significance and purpose. God expects me to use the investment He's entrusted to me in my abilities, talents, personality, and creative potential.

The pain and heartache of my life serve an eternal purpose and will be transformed at our final redemption in Jesus Christ.

God has uniquely designed and positioned me to carry out His purposes in the world. I'm His masterpiece, not just His servant.

God's purpose is for me to experience joy in fulfilling the purposes He's called me to.

I am blessed with God's assurance of a future and a hope that God is working for my best interests and His ultimate glory in all circumstances.

As God's child, I bring Him profound pleasure and joy.

I am blessed with joy in obedience, knowing it brings pleasure to God.

I am called to develop each part of my being and walk in wholeness, overcoming brokenness and bringing my gifts to full fruition.

MY PROVISION

I'm blessed with God's immeasurable spiritual resources and provision in every area of my life, including my deepest heartaches and needs.

I'm blessed with the leading of the Holy Spirit to respond to my problems in faith, not with a victim mentality, avoidance, blame-shifting, or rationalization.

I am blessed with wisdom, perseverance, endurance, and joy as I face problems, rejoicing in the situations of my life instead of complaining and turning back as I find new treasures in the nature of God.

Through the power of the Holy Spirit, I'm enabled to embrace problems, view them as challenges and opportunities for growing faith, as new ways to see the facets of God and how He will work in and through them to accomplish His plan for my life.

I can see the presence of God in problems and can look in faith beyond the immediate to the eternal.

I am blessed with discernment to see things from God's perspective as I'm led by the Holy Spirit.

As an heir of God and a joint heir with Jesus Christ, I lack nothing emotionally, physically, mentally, spiritually, practically, or in any way.

The Spirit of God indwells me as His sanctuary and makes known to me the joy of God's presence.

God provides me with perfect peace in spite of my circumstances or others' attitudes or actions toward me.

I can know joy that transcends pain.

God communicates to me personally through His Spirit and His Word, and I can be confident that even in the silences He is always communing and will speak again in the right time and place.

God's timing is at work in all things, and I can trust Him to arrive, provide, communicate, and change things at exactly the right time.

I can trust God's faithfulness. He's always moved at exactly the right time in the past and will continue to do so in the future.

I move my Father's heart with joy when my spirit responds to the Holy Spirit and when I take on the character of Christ.

MY PROTECTION

I am blessed with God's security and intervention as He rescues me from the trap of the Enemy designed to destroy me.

I know the favor of God and freedom from anxiety and fear, aware that each moment of my life is Father-filtered.

I am blessed by experiences of God's "pruning" in order that I will bring forth more fruit in the seasons of my life.

I'm comforted and assured in knowing that God takes situations that Satan intends for my harm and turns them into powerful experiences for my good.

I am blessed with unshakable confidence that God is in charge of my circumstances.

I'm bound eternally to my Father in love—nothing in heaven, hell, or on earth can separate me from His love.

I'm blessed with freedom from fear of man and an unhealthy fear of God.

MY POSITION

I'm blessed with complete forgiveness for my sins through the work of Jesus Christ on the cross.

I have an intimate relationship with Jesus Christ and access to God the Father through the work of the Holy Spirit.

When God looks at me, He sees only a sinless, perfect child.

I have immediate, intimate access to God at any moment of my life.

I am a child of God, led by His Spirit and blessed with a mindset of sonship.

I am blessed with the gift of knowing peace with God, with myself, and with others through the work of Jesus Christ in eradicating my sins and repairing my brokenness.

I am loved by God with the same love He has for Jesus.

MY POWER

I'm empowered to bring peace to a world in darkness.

The joy of the Lord is my strength.

God has blessed me with strength to accomplish what He has called me to do because I'm able to drink deeply of the joy the Father has placed in me, His handiwork, for His purposes.

I am blessed with the power of the Holy Spirit to live at peace with even my enemies.

Through the work of the Holy Spirit, I am blessed with an ability to understand the Word of God and its principles and to receive direction from the Spirit specific to my life.

I am blessed with a spirit that is sensitive to discern right from wrong and a desire to experience the peace and pleasure of God.

I am blessed with the light and life of Jesus living in and through me.

I am blessed with dominion over the powers of darkness.

Acknowledgments

My heartfelt thanks to Gary Heim, who has counseled and walked beside Dan and me over the past four years. Gary's insights have helped me explore my deceptive self-talk and guided me down a path of transformed thinking.

Thank you to the life-changing teaching ministry of Blythefield Hills Baptist Church and its culture of transparency, accountability, and discipleship.

My deep thanks, warm hugs, and offerings of dark chocolate seafoam to the Guild, my dear writing sisters who infuse me with energy, creativity, joy, and love in the bond of Christ—Julie Johnson, Lorilee Craker, Ann Byle, Sharon Carrns, Angela Blycker, Cynthia Beach, Alison Hodgson, and Tracy Groot.

Sincere thanks to the amazing team at Moody Publishers who had a vision for this book.

As always and most importantly, buckets and buckets of love, gratitude, admiration, and praise for my husband, Dan, who's patiently and selflessly given to me out of an overflow of neverending love. He's experienced the power of my self-talk—the ugly, and the redeemed—and cheered me on through every soul change. I am a woman truly blessed.

THE UNCOMMON WOMAN

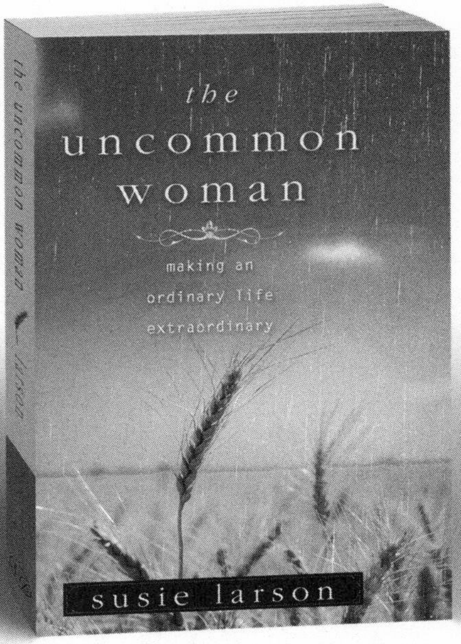

ISBN-13: 978-0-8024-5279-5

This book is for the woman who longs to rise up out of the stereotypical behavior of gossip, insecurity, pettiness, and small dreams. She has an unfulfilled desire to be someone who goes against the grain of the common for the sole purpose of living a life with conviction. The woman who reads this book is ready to believe in her deep value, ready to accept her high calling, and ready to make a difference in a world in need of her influence.

Find out more about author Susie Larson by visiting:
www.susielarson.com | susielarsonblog.typepad.com

MOODY PUBLISHERS.

1-800-678-8812 · MOODYPUBLISHERS.COM

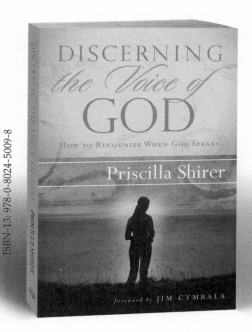